LEA SKILLS FOR THE NURSE MANAGER

Restructuring the Role of Management in Today's Healthcare Setting

LEADERSHIP SKILLS FOR THE NURSE MANAGER

Restructuring the Role of Management in Today's Healthcare Setting

KATHLEEN O'SULLIVAN MOTT

IRWIN
Professional Publishing®
Burr Ridge, Illinois
New York, New York

◥◤ **Times Mirror**
◣ **Higher Education Group**

Library of Congress Cataloging-in-Publication Data

Mott, Kathleen O'Sullivan, 1930–
     Leadership skills for the nurse manager : restructuring the role of management in today's healthcare setting / Kathleen O'Sullivan Mott.
          p.   cm.
     Includes index.
     ISBN 0-7863-0860-5
     1. Nursing services—Personnel management.   2. Nursing services—Administration.   I. Title.
     RT89.3.M68   1996
     362.1'73'0683—dc20   96–7876

Printed in the United States of America
1 2 3 4 5 6 7 8 9 0   ML   3 2 1 0 9 8 7 6

This book is dedicated to:
My husband, Larry Bruce Mott
My best friend, my love, and my life.

INTRODUCTION: OR, WHY SHOULD I READ THIS BOOK?

Once upon a time in healthcare, and especially in nursing, we expected a long-term relationship with our employers. Nurses gave of themselves to their patients and their employers, patients expressed gratitude to "my nurse," and as long as we did exactly what our patients and employers wanted us to do we were rewarded with an informal tenure system. As a general rule longevity translated into job security. This structure was basically authoritarian, however, and today we would call that "codependency." As nurses we were naturals for this phenomenon; after all, didn't we get into this profession because we wanted to help people? Of course we did . . . it's what made us such superb caregivers.

To make life even more complex for us as nurses, we began life as the product of the marriage between the military and religion. This history is noted for its "command-and-control" style of management: very paternalistic; denying decision making to any but the higher echelons; a follow-my-orders-and-I'll-take-care-of-you model of management; a style guaranteed to produce a rigid, inefficient system, inflexible staff, and to reinforce that same codependency.

Healthcare reform, accomplished mainly in the private sector, has brought about massive changes in the management of hospitals, home health agencies, physician office practices—anywhere we are likely to find practitioners skilled in the art and science of patient care. The "art and science of patient care" is now the "art, science, and *business* of patient care."

Codependence is *out*, command and control is *out;* interdependence is *in.* Our employers expect an empowered, flexible, motivated, responsible, and diverse workforce committed to a philosophy of quality and to employee accountability. While the goal of quality patient care with measurable outcomes and a reasonable cost remains intact, how we reach that goal is changing dramatically. Career paths are nontraditional; today's job or position might not exist tomorrow.

Michael Hammer and James Champy, considered by many to be the grandfathers of the reengineering phenomenon, flatly state that "when a process is reengineered, jobs evolve from narrow and task-oriented to multidimensional. People who once did as they were instructed now make choices and decisions on their own instead." (*Reengineering the Corporation*. New York: HarperCollins Business, 1994, p. 65.) Caregiving, nurturing, and dependence are yesterday's models . . . interdependence is the model for today and tomorrow.

An interdependent workforce requires a manager with skills far different from the authoritarian, paternalistic manager of yesterday. Today's manager must possess the knowledge, ability, skills, and motivation to foster a love of learning, decision making, participation, flexibility, accountability, and responsibility in her staff.[1]

We do not have the privilege of tinkering with the edges of the role we now have; we are obliged to throw it out and to redraw, reengineer, and restructure the role of the nurse manager.

That's what this book is all about: redrawing, reengineering, and restructuring the role of today's nurse manager.

---

1. OK, let's get this out of the way now. Women represent 90 percent of the nursing profession; therefore, the appropriate pronoun is "she." For those who insist on equality, I shall refer to physicians as "he" even though half of new physicians are now female. Besides, this s/he stuff is clumsy, and I have a problem with mixing the singular and plural by using "individual" and "they."
   Having said that, let's get on with the good stuff!

PROLOGUE

In order to provide nurses with a new model of management, we must first provide a conceptual framework. Having done that, our next task is to fill that framework with principles derived from a variety of theories, all of which tie neatly together to justify our actions and support the conceptual framework. This book is designed to accomplish that complex purpose.

The conceptual framework is drawn from Dororthea Orem's self-care concept of nursing, wherein our legitimate role as a nurse is defined as doing for the person only those things the person would do for herself if she had the knowledge, ability, skills, and motivation (*Nursing: Concepts of Practice.* New York: McGraw-Hill, 1971). Self-care is an action theory that presupposes decision making. This concept lends itself nicely to management in general, and today's nurse manager role in particular.

Eight principles, also derived from theory, support this conceptual framework. They are:

Principle 1: Most people want to live up to our expectations.

We'll look at a model of management/leadership that encourages us to be firm and specific about our expectations. We will not ask that anyone read our minds, primarily because even if they wanted to, they couldn't.

Principle 2: Interaction with others is more effective when we meet them where they are rather than where we want them to be.

It's another way of saying, "I accept you as you are (even though that isn't necessarily the way I want you to be)." This same model will help us to identify the level of functioning of our staff, and will provide us with the flexibility we must have when we're working with today's diverse work group.

Principle 3: Given the knowledge, ability, skills, and motivation, people can make their own decisions in matters pertaining to their work.

What truly provides the thrust for motivation? What simply provides for satisfaction? There really is more to motivation than the insights provided by Abraham Maslow, whose framework provides a foundation for us. We're going to add expectancy theory to Maslow's hierarchy of motivational needs.

Principle 4: We can't change anyone's behavior but our own.

We'll take another look at motivation, adding a dimension to what we already know. Then we'll look at a method of problem solving that incorporates these motivational concepts within the framework of behavior modification.

Principle 5: Any effort to implement change will be met by a degree of resistance proportional to the meaning of the change to the person.

It's no longer a matter of, "Are we going to change?" It is the "change du jour." How can we apply this principle and what we know about people, organizations, and motivation to the world of constant change we find ourselves in today? We're going to look at that. A major new role for the nurse manager is that of "coach." We also add some of the basic principles of adult learning to our general principles and examine how they work, both when we are in the midst of change and in our everyday world of management (although today it seems like being in the midst of change *is* the everyday world of management).

Principle 6: Communication is most effective when the speaker and the audience speak the same language.

This wouldn't be a book about management if there weren't a chapter on communication. Never one to disappoint . . . it's here. I've put the communication wheel in the book; you remember . . . the sender, encoder, interpreter, receiver thing. I actually included it so that you would know that I know it . . . *so do you!* We're going to add several dimensions to what we already know about communication. Then, and *only* then, we're going to spend some time looking at upward communications, or, "how to get those above me to hear me when they really don't want to hear what I have to say."

Principle 7: Most people who are difficult to deal with are responding to their own anger or fear.

If everyone were cooperative and easy to get along with, our lives would be simple and the book could end here. Unfortunately, about 20 percent of the individuals with whom we interact are difficult to get along with, and this small group consumes about 80 percent of our time and energy.

We'll examine the dynamics underlying the behavior of the angry, aggressive person, and the whiny, fearful, manipulative person. Then we'll discuss effective ways of dealing with each one so that we can reclaim some of that time and energy.

Principle 8: When an irresistible force meets an immovable object in a clash of two personalities, the most effective resolution is when both parties get something out of it.

We are *not* going to solve their problem for them, even though we may jolly well think that we know what it is. There is a process, a structure, within which the opposing forces can solve their *own* problem. Far more effective. We provide the structure . . . they provide the definition of the problem and the solution.

Several leaders in nursing agreed to be interviewed for this book. I'd like to introduce them to you now:

June C. Bowman, M.S.N., R.N.
Vice President of Nursing
Centennial Medical Center
Nashville, Tennessee

Frances McG. Edwards, M.S.N., R.N.
Principle, Health Futures, Inc.
Past President, Tennessee Nurses Association
Nashville, Tennessee

Judith M. Jenkins, M.S.N., R.N.
Case Manager, Trauma Unit
Vanderbilt University Medical Center
Nashville, Tennessee

Jean T. Johnson, M.S., R.N.
Organizational Development
Saint Thomas Hospital
Nashville, Tennessee

Mary Lou Jones, Ph.D., R.N.
Vice President, Patient Care Services and Women's Services
Pennsylvania Hospital
Philadelphia, Pennsylvania

John C. McDonald, M.S., R.N.
Vice President, Clinical Systems Development
Tennessee Community Health, LLC
Brentwood, Tennessee

Judith B. Prater, B.S.N., R.N.
Home Health Agency
Wichita, Kansas

Each one of these leaders has made significant contributions to nursing in his or her own way. All were gracious enough to agree to an interview during which I sought their insight into their own effectiveness and successes—a daunting task!

These nursing leaders will be identified by an asterisk as they are mentioned throughout the book to remind us that they are real people. All other characters in the book (with the exception of the author) are imaginary. Any resemblance to any person, living or dead, is purely coincidental.

Start anywhere in the book you wish. Jump around from chapter to chapter, if you see something of particular interest. I ask, however, that you understand and accept that each chapter builds on the knowledge, ability, and skills gained in the preceding chapters.

Have fun. And, blessings upon each one of us as we embark on this latest challenge.

Kathleen O'Sullivan Mott

ACKNOWLEDGMENTS

The presence of one name as the author on the title page of a book is misleading. Many people contribute, in countless and often unseen ways. Some of the important players in the development of this book include:

My family, whose belief in me and support for me are constants in my life: Larry B. Mott, Bruce T. Mott, David P. Mott, Larry K. Mott, John K. Mott, Chris K. Mott, Susan Neese, Nancy Jones, Anne Chambers, and Jane Patrick. Each one offered significant support in his or her own way. John and Chris did yeoman duty with their computer support.

Shelley Wilmoth, whose comments on the structure and content in the first drafts were consistently on target.

The nurse leaders who believe so strongly in the future role of the nurse manager that they gave generously of their time for interviews: June Bowman, Frances Edwards, Judy Jenkins, Jean Johnson, Mary Lou Jones, John McDonald, and Judy Prater.

The staff at Irwin Professional Publishing, especially Bev Orr, Kris Rynne, Patrick Muller, Cindy Ledwith, and Denise Santor-Mitzit.

And, the thousands of nurse managers, from charge nurse to administrator, with whom I've had the privilege of interacting. Each one has made a contribution, and collectively, they have strengthened my belief system.

TABLE OF
CONTENTS

**Introduction
(Or, Why Should I Read This Book?)**   vii

Preface   ix

Chapter 1

**The Vision
In Which We Establish the Framework   1**

Level One: The Foundation: Tell My Role: Authoritarian/Directive   3
    Where Do We Fit In?   6
    What's in It for the Staff Member?   7
    Boundaries   7
    Decision Making   8
Level Two Sell: Knowledge, Ability, and Skills My Role:
Teach/Coach   10
    Boundaries   11
    Decision Making   12
Level Three Participation My Role: Support   13
    Decision Making   14
    Boundaries   15
Level Four Delegate My Role: Be a Resource   18
    Why Should We Delegate?   18
    Reasons Not to Delegate   19
    How Do We Delegate?   20
    What to Delegate   21
    What Not to Delegate   21
    Boundaries   24
    Decision Making   24
    A Look at Ourselves   25
    A Look at Our Staff   26

Chapter 2

Applying the Vision in the Real World
Should We Redirect, or Reprimand? 29

Chapter 3

Motivation 201
Or, How Do I Get Them to Do What I Need to Have Done
Because They Want to? 41

How Did We Get Here . . . and Where Are We? 41
The Satisfiers, or *Dis*satisfiers 43
The Motivators 44
Self-Actualization, or Achievement 46
    Analysis and Discussion 48
    Additional Thoughts about Motivation 49
Expectancy Theory 49
    Notes 56

Chapter 4

Behavior Motivation
In Which We Modify Someone's Behavior 57

Principles and Practice 57
Application of the Process 71

Chapter 5

Change, Change, Change
In Which We Dissect the Principles and Practice of Change 75

    First: The Personal Process of Change 76
How to Accomplish Change with the Least Pain 77
Structure 79
    What 79
    Why? 81
    When? 84
    How 86
    Where 87

Who   *88*

Take a Stress Break   *91*

Knowledge, Ability, and Skills   92

Role of the Teacher   92

Application of Principles   96

    Second: A Model Of Organizational Change   *96*

    *Third: Intersection of Personal and Organizational Models
of Change*   *99*

A Successful Change   101

A Disastrous Change   103

Chapter 6

The Art and Science of Language Skills
The Mandatory Chapter on Communications   107

The Parent-Adult-Child Model of Communication   108

    *Why Is the Parent-Adult-Child Model of Communication
Important?*   *110*

    Kinds of Transactions   *113*

Listening   119

    Why All This Emphasis on Listening?   *120*

    Factors Affecting My Ability to Listen   *120*

    Selective Actions by Listeners   *122*

    Skills to Help with Active Listening   *124*

    Danger! Danger! Danger!   *128*

Upward Communication   130

The Decision-Making Process   131

    *Getting the Attention of My Administrator When I Have
a Problem*   *133*

Chapter 7

Difficult People
In Which We Discuss the 20% of People Who Cause 80% of Our Headaches 139

Anger   140

    Continuum of Behaviors Used to Express Anger   *142*

    Anger and Ourselves   *149*

Confronting an Aggressive Attack   154
How to Construct an Assertive Message   155
"You" Is a Four-Letter Word!   159
The Beginner with Assertiveness   160
Manipulation   162
The Victim   169
The Extremes to Which Manipulators Go   172
Summary of Helpful Hints   173

Chapter 8

Conflict Resolution
When the Irresistible Force Meets the Immovable Object   175

What Is a Conflict and Where Does It Come From?   175
Personality Clashes   178
Conflict Resolution   178
Method of Choice   180
The Conflict-Resolution Process   181
Pat and Becky: A One-Act Play   183

Epilogue
Or, What Now?   191

Where Do I Go from Here?   193

Bibliography   195

Index   199

About the Author   206

CHAPTER

The Vision

In Which We Establish the Framework

Dorothea Orem has provided us with just the conceptual framework we need to apply the eight prinicples for development of an interdependent staff. She calls it *self-care*. Orem says, essentially, that I care enough about you to do for you *only* those things that you would do for yourself if you had the knowledge, ability, skills, and motivation. This truly raises caring to a higher level because it is frequently easier to do *for* another person rather than taking the time and effort to teach them to do it themselves. Whereas Orem addressed patient care, I have brought this theory with me to the management of multiple persons within an organizational system. The eight principles that support our conceptual framework are derived from theories representing a variety of disciplines: nursing, personality development, psychology, organizational development, and others. They will guide us in establishing, developing, and maintaining a highly functional, interdependent staff.

Great! How do we put that together so that all the pieces fit and are understandable, and *doable*? I'm going to use the analogy of a building a house within which all the residents can be as creative as they want to be with their activities because they all know exactly what must be done to keep the house running in an orderly fashion. The residents have the knowledge, ability, and skills to tend to each other and the house. They are motivated to participate in the care and feeding of each other and the house. And, they have a sense of achievement that their activities are important and serve to improve the lives of the residents and the status of the house.

All houses must have a good foundation. We provide a foundation when we articulate very clearly what the expectations are for maintaining a residency in this house. When we begin climbing the steps to the first floor we find that we need to increase, or add to, our knowledge, ability, and skills. Having acquired the knowledge, ability, and skills, we are now motivated to practice these new skills. Having had a secure environment within which to practice these new skills, we're ready to make decisions and to take action independently (or interdependently), to go it alone within certain boundaries. By using this framework of taking one step at a time, our staff are encouraged to be the most creative, independent, self-satisfying selves they can be, within the limitations imposed on us by the structure within the organization within which we find ourselves. When we get through building the house it will look like this, and we will be assured of ease of movement between the levels.

In fact, Hersey and Blanchard have provided us with a four-level model of situational leadership (*Management of Organizational Behavior*, 4th ed. Englewood Cliffs, NJ: Prentice-Hall, 1982) that meets our needs perfectly.

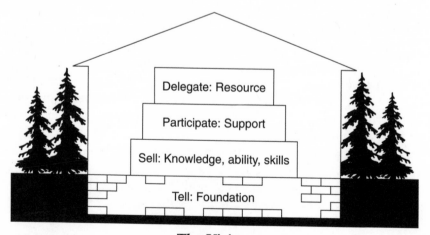

The Vision

LEVEL ONE:
TELL: THE FOUNDATION
My Role: Authoritarian/Directive

Principle 1: Most people want to live up to our expectations.

We must let our staff know what our expectations are. We must provide them with a sound, solid, and firm foundation. I can't emphasize this too much. *It is the single most important function we have as managers. Without a firm foundation, the rest of it doesn't matter.*

This is a very authoritarian role, very directive, and very appropriate. We hear quite frequently that we are not to be "authoritarian"; we are to be "participative." *We can't be participative until we have provided the foundation within which it is possible to be participative.*

Principle 2: Interaction with others is more effective when we meet them where they are rather than where we want them to be.

Mission Statement, Philosophy, Values

Every new staff member (and every seasoned staff member who is new to us) must know who we are as an organization, what purpose is served by our existence, what we hope to accomplish, and what our values are. It is equally important that we describe who *we* are and what *our* values are. How do we fit into the organization's mission? What can that staff member reasonably expect of us? What do we expect of the staff member?

These building blocks, fit together carefully, make up the foundation.

There are many analogies and examples in our history and our literature to support the need for a firm foundation. I remember taking my children to Sunday school and listening to the teacher tell the parable of the man who built his house on sand and the man who built his house on rocks. Or the Christian hymn "How Firm the Foundation." Or the fairy tale of the three little pigs, and whether they would build their house of sticks or of bricks. Our intent is to "build our house of bricks," to go far beyond the job description. The mission statement is an articulation of the core set of values, beliefs, and attitudes that guide us as an organization. It also includes our role as a manager, the staff member's role, and her importance to the organization. It is a vision of who we are, what we want to be, how we are going to get there, how we fit into that big picture, and why we're doing what we're doing.

*Frances McG. Edwards, M.S.N., R.N., attributes much of her success to her emphasis on establishing a solid foundation. She said:

> One of the reasons is that I value everybody, regardless of who they are. I don't know that there is anyone from whom I haven't learned something, so I always start out by giving them the feeling that I value them, which I do.
>
> The other thing is that I try to share more of myself so that others feel that I am a part of the process. I think that this ability to share ourselves with others comes with experience. We have to be comfortable with ourselves before we can share our feelings, experiences, and vulnerabilities.

Job Description   The job description is important. Our staff must know what we expect them to do; how we want it done; by what standards they will be held accountable; when we want it done; where we want it done; how we'll know when it's been done, and the rewards; and, how we'll know it hasn't been done, and the consequences.

Policies and Procedures   Policies and procedures are an important part of this foundation. It is not fair to hold someone responsible without their knowing what they're responsibilities are. Beyond this, we must be able to articulate a vision that says this is who I am as an individual, and this is what you can expect of me.

Strong Leaders   Think about presidents who have been strong leaders. We're not talking about politics now, we're talking about *leadership*. Harry Truman was viewed and esteemed as a strong leader, as was Ronald Reagan. What did they have in common? *We always knew where they stood!* Other recent presidents have not been viewed as strong leaders. What did they have in common? *We had some doubts about where they stood . . . We weren't sure they meant what they said. They seemed to say one thing today and another tomorrow.*

We have all worked, at one time or another, for or with someone whom we didn't particularly like. We enjoyed working with or for them, though, because we "always knew where they stood." Our goal is not to be liked; it is to be respected.

There is a woman in my community with whom I have worked on several projects. We don't particularly like each other; however, we work well together. We make a heck of a team because each one brings different strengths to the table. Individually, each one of us is good in a particular area; together, we're dynamite. When the project is over we go our separate ways . . . until time for the next project.

Look at the accompanying mission statement for what it really says.

MISSION STATEMENT

MYTH O'LOGIC HEALTHCARE CENTER

We believe that our mission in serving the healthcare needs of the community is:

To promote an interfaith community in the spirit of equality and respect for humankind.

To respect and to preserve the dignity of each and every person we serve.

To maintain a viable, dynamic organization that strives for excellence.

To provide an environment within which those we serve can reach their highest mental, physical, and spiritual potential.

To support the family.

To maintain fiscal practices that reflect concern for those we serve: the patient, physician, employee, family, stockholders, and community.

Analysis.   What does this mission statement tell us about the organization? What would I, as a manager, say to the new staff member?

1. We believe that a spiritual life is important; however, the particular expression of that spirituality, or lack of it, is up to the individual.

2. We respect the dignity of each person as demonstrated in our efforts to ensure that each person is empowered to function at her highest possible level within the constraints imposed by the organization.

3. Dynamic organizations are organizations designed to adapt to the changing conditions of the world in which we live. That means that we expect our staff to be flexible and ready to change with us.

4. We recognize the knowledge explosion. Keeping up with new knowledge requires constant learning. We are prepared to support, with education, our patients and staff in their efforts to reach their highest potential, and we expect our patients and staff to participate willingly in educational efforts designed to keep up with the knowledge explosion.

5. We support family values. We make every effort to maintain flexibility in staffing to ensure that families are able to spend time together. When that flexibility is impossible due to circumstances beyond our control, we expect our staff to be understanding and to remember that our basic purpose is to serve the patient.

6. Organizations that do not practice sound fiscal management do not survive. We cannot serve our patients, physicians, staff, the stockholders, or the community without closely guarding our resources and ensuring that revenues exceed costs. (Not-for-profit agencies might not have to please stockholders. They do, however, have to ensure that revenues exceed costs or they don't survive. Hence, the oft quoted saying, "No margin, no mission.")

Where Do We Fit In?

As nurses, we are the primary providers of patient care. We are the lynchpin when it comes to putting the mission statement into practice.

We consistently include an assessment of the patient's spiritual dimension in the plan of care, or critical path, because we respect the power of that belief system in the patient's ability to achieve the highest potential possible in matters pertaining to health.

We respect the dignity of the individual by application of management principles designed to empower staff and patients to make their own decisions, within the limitations imposed by illness or by legal or organizational constraints.

We accept that an organization must be able and willing to change in order to survive. We are flexible and willing to adapt to new knowledge and improved ways of serving our customer, the patient.

We are ready and willing to continue learning, and to encourage others to continue their learning for mental, physical, and spiritual growth.

We are mindful of limited resources and that there is "no free lunch."

What's in It for the Staff Member?

Active participation in putting into action the beliefs expressed in the mission statement ensures that the staff member will be able to achieve at a level consistent with mutually agreed-upon goals, whether that goal is delivering patient care at a highly personal level, focusing on the efficiency of the system as a case manager, or advancing to a management position.

Boundaries

Wherever we are, and whatever our roles, we all have boundaries. When we are establishing a firm foundation for our staff member, we maintain very tight control; we limit movement; we follow up very closely to see to it that the employee understands and accepts the boundaries. This is very appropriate for a beginning staff member.

There are, after all, rules and regulations we must adhere to to ensure that the mission of the organization, as expressed in the goals and objectives, are met, and to ensure that the pieces within the organization work together for the benefit of the patient. While we honor the individual and the family, our first concern is the patient. Another way of saying this is that while we provide infant and child care, and adult day care for frail elderly family members, at the same time we expect dependable attendance, adherence to the policies and procedures as outlined by Human Resources, willing performance of those responsibilities outlined in the job description, and achievement of agreed-upon standards.

Decision Making

When we are managing at the *tell* level, we make all the decisions. That's appropriate for a short period of time because we must be sure that the new staff member can function within the constraints present in any organization, and those that might be uniquely present in this organization.

> The manager,
>
> manager,
>
> A leader must be.
>
> That's Most
>
> Important,
>
> As we all can see.
>
> —*Winnie the Pooh*
>
> (Roger E. Allen)

The problem with keeping all the decision making is that we also keep all the responsibility. That was difficult when we had 8 to 25 employees; it is just about impossible with a span of control that includes 60 or more employees. More important than keeping the decision making and responsibility is the result of those actions. When we make all the decisions, we foster dependency in our employees and they, in turn, begin to hate us because of that dependency.

We hear comments such as, "It isn't my fault; that's the way Katie said she wanted it done." We also can't sleep at night because we wake up at 2:00 AM wondering if we remembered to tell John to be sure to contact the patient representative about the glasses left behind when Mrs. Jones was discharged. Did we remember to tell Susan that Mrs. Chambers is expecting her home visit at 7:00 AM rather than the previously scheduled 8:00 AM appointment. Or, did anyone tell Dr. Neese to plan on a long day tomorrow?

Staff who are reasonably competent and independent will, after a short period of time, begin to let us know that we need to "loosen up," "turn loose," "back off." Generally, it's comments such as, "I know, I know. You don't have to remind me again." Or, it could be body language . . . waving a hand behind a hip, as if to say, "Go away."

Managers with strong control needs will have difficulty turning loose. After all, we've been making the decisions for years. Even though we *know* that today's reengineered organization demands pushing the decision making down to the frontline worker, we just aren't accustomed to letting the other person have any power! This is the origin of "micromanagement," the inability to turn loose. I've seen micromanagers run off very competent nurses because those nurses simply weren't able to function with a manager breathing down their necks.

We have applied the first two principles. For the new employee we have met the person where she is; in need of a firm foundation. At the same time we have stated our expectations, clearly and distinctly.

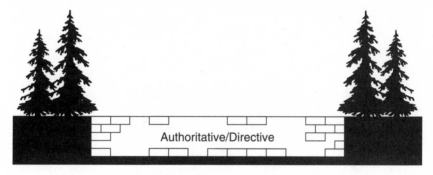

The Foundation: Tell

The structure is now in place for the staff member to embark on the road of achievement and accountability, given the constraints of our organization, limited only by her lack of knowledge, ability, skills, motivation, and practice. That person is now ready for another level of functioning, and ready for a different style of management from us.

Note: If the new employee complains about the values, beliefs, and attitude of this organization, as expressed in the mission statement and in policies and procedures, throughout the traditional 90-day probationary period, *let the employee go! She is never going to be happy!* Better to end the pain and let her find a place of employment more to her liking.

A little insight: The *R* in nuRse stands for "rescue." We are professional rescuers. If we honestly, truly believe, at the bottom of our hearts, that if we just try harder we can get that person turned around; *if we have to try one more time;* then extend the probation another 90 days. Resist the temptation to convert the person to an accepted FTE.

LEVEL TWO
SELL: KNOWLEDGE, ABILITY, AND SKILLS
My Role: Teach/Coach

Principle 3: Given the knowledge, ability, skills, and motivation, people can make their own decisions in matters pertaining to their work.

Up to this point our staff have been passive recipients of what we have been "telling" them. It is now incumbent upon us to attempt to get them to "buy into" our mission so that it might become "their" mission. We must also ensure that they have the knowledge, ability, and skills necessary to fulfill that mission.

There it is. They have to know how to do whatever we expect them to do. It is our job to assess their level of knowledge, ability, and skill as these components impact on their level of functioning.

What are we looking for?

- We do not expect the patient care assistant to function at the same level as the registered nurse because she doesn't have the knowledge base.
- We don't expect the registered nurse to be able to delegate to the patient care assistant when she has never delegated and doesn't understand the delegation process.
- We don't expect the registered nurse to be able to design and implement critical paths without classes designed to meet her need for a new understanding of this organized patient care delivery system.
- We don't expect to be able to develop a zero-based budget if we've never done one before and don't have the foggiest notion of where to start and what it should look like when we get done.
- We don't expect our staff to make independent decisions when they have, to this point, been required to seek permission before taking action of any consequence.

Whereas we weren't much interested in whether or not our staff agreed with us when we were operating at the *tell* level, now we do care. We were very task oriented, and not too interested in the relationship at the *tell* level. There is an assumption now that our staff understands and accepts the mission, goals, objectives of this organization. Moving beyond that, it is now important to us that our staff understand "why" we believe that one method is superior to another, or "why" we do something a particular way, or "why" we consider one source of knowledge to be preferable to another. We are moving into a role that says the relationship is important. We seek input from our staff and consider their learned judgment in the decision-making process.

Anytime something new happens we find ourselves at *sell*. That is, assuming that the foundation is solid. We can all remember one change in our professional lives; when we, as new graduates, experienced "reality shock." The foundation, as the organization explained it to us, was solid. We just knew that we were going to be able to practice nursing the way we were taught in school even though our new employers valiantly attempted to get us to understand that it was different in the real world. We did eventually adjust to the reality of health care as compared and contrasted with the academic world of nursing—but it took some real understanding and help from our nurse managers!

This is where we concentrate on staff development needs. We can't afford to make assumptions. Here are some examples of some of the issues to be addressed in *sell*.

Anytime new knowledge, ability, or skills are needed, our staff is at *sell*, and that's where we meet them; that's where our interactions with them will be the most effective. Our responsibility is to see to it that we teach or coach them in the new concepts or skills, or that we provide the resources needed for their learning.

Today's literature is replete with books and articles on the "learning organization" and the necessity for the manager to be a "coach." Given the rapid pace of change we're experiencing, I have no doubt that we will be spending a lot of time at this level for the next several years.

Anytime we are in a teaching mode, we are in *sell*. When we attempt to "sell" the other person on a new or different concept, thought, way of doing things, we are at *sell*. This says that the relationship is important; otherwise, I would simply say, "Do it," as I did in the *tell* level.

Boundaries

Our staff now has a much larger playing field. We don't watch so closely. While we constantly assess for the needed knowledge, ability, and skills, we also encourage them to do the tasks, to do it themselves. We recognize their "approximate rights." In other words, they don't *have* to do what we are requesting; they respond positively to our requests because they *want* to.

> If everyone is thinking alike then somebody isn't thinking.
>
> —George S. Patton, Jr.

Decision Making

Whereas we made decisions without necessarily including staff input when we were managing at the *tell* level, we now actively seek and include their input in our decision-making process. While we are still making the decisions, staff have the ability to cause us to modify those decisions, or even to change them.

The Decision-Making Process

As a part of the process, we teach decsion-making skills by example and by coaching.

Kerrigan has provided us with a guide that will greatly assist us in this process [Kerrigan, K. "Decision Making in Today's Complex Environment." *Nursing Administration Quarterly* 15, no. 4 (1991):1–5]. The steps in the decision-making process include:

1. Agreement on the goals and objectives.
2. A search for alternatives, *supported with objective data.*
3. Evaluation and comparison of the alternatives, *accompanied with strengths and weaknesses of each of the alternatives.*
4. Selection of an alternative, *with the rationale for that selection.*
5. Implementation of the decision.
6. Evaluation of the effectiveness of the decision.

The place to start with this process is in our being prepared to support our opinions and decisions with objective data, as well as expecting this same action from our staff.

We are adding depth to our levels; they are beginning to appear as if ascending to a higher level has a purpose, and the levels look like they do in the accompanying drawing.

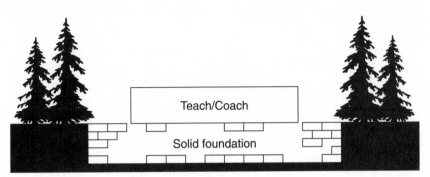

Building on a Solid Foundation: Sell

Given that the foundation is solid and the staff person has the requisite knowledge, ability, and skills to be able to get the job done, that person is now ready to *participate*, and our role is to move with her.

Note: Persons who are insecure by their very natures are inclined to get stuck at the *sell* level. They may indeed have the knowledge, ability, and skills; they are simply fearful of using them. We've all had staff members with whom our interactions seemed to focus on figuratively cupping our hands under their bottoms and attempting to shove them out of the nest, like a baby robin. We've heard ourselves saying, "You can do it. Go ahead. You can do it. Just *try*."

LEVEL THREE
PARTICIPATION
My Role: Support

Given that our staff person has a solid foundation, understands and supports the mission of our organization and the constraints imposed by policies and procedures, and has the knowledge, ability, and skills to achieve her potential, she is now ready to try those skills in a supportive environment. Our major responsibility is to *support the staff person as she gets out there and puts into practice her knowledge and skills.* Is she going to be perfect in all that she does? No, of course not. That's an unreasonable expectation. There will be successes, there will be failures, and there will be aborted attempts.

Decision Making

While some of us may *never* have made a dumb decision, I have made a few. In fact, some of my best learning came about as the result of dumb decisions. I call them "significant learning experiences." Some of them were so significant I only had to learn them once. With others I was a little slow to get the message and had to learn that particular lesson several times.

Adults simply learn best when they do it themselves.

One of the reasons we like experienced staff and managers is that they've had the time and opportunity to make those important dumb decisions. They've also had time for trial and error in practicing new skills. Precious few of us come out of a learning situation as experts. Most of us need the time, encouragement, and freedom to practice.

> Some of the best learning comes from dumb decisions.

These days, with change happening so rapidly, we can't afford to sit on the sidelines and moan that we've always done it that way. In fact, no less a management guru than Tom Peters has said, "We need lots more of it. We need faster failure" (*Thriving on Chaos*. New York: HarperCollins, 1987). Hammer and Champy had this to say:

> A task-oriented, traditional company hires people and expects them to follow the rules. Companies that have reengineered don't want employees who can follow rules; they want people who will make their own rules" (p. 70).

How do we encourage people to make dumb decisions?

Trust. The single most important element in the participative, dumb decision, experience is the trust the staff person *must* have that it's OK to make a mistake, that we truly value the benefits of learning by experience, and that the world as we know it really will not come to an end.

The obstacle here: William J. Morin, in his book *Silent Sabotage,* reports that up to 75 percent of employees don't trust their managers (New York. American Management Association, 1995). His own study confirmed that 45 percent of the human resource executives interviewed believe that most employees distrust their managers. Even more damning is that while 67 percent (two out of three) of the employees thought that a *stated* code of values was prevalent, *only 7 percent* (fewer than 1 in 10) think that we actually *live* by them. We will never get staff to "make mistakes faster" if they don't trust us. We establish that trust in the *tell* level.

Boundaries

The second step we must take is to establish the boundary within which the staff person can make a decision. Not fair to encourage decision making and then to announce that she didn't have the authority to make that decision. That's like sending someone out on a limb and chopping the limb off after her. Trust *me;* that doesn't build a trusting relationship.

Let's look at the accompanying case study.

C A S E   S T U D Y

MYTH O'LOGIC HEALTHCARE CENTER

The Myth O'Logic Healthcare Center, following an intensive investigation, and with considerable input from Nursing Service, has implemented a case management model of patient care. This represents a radical change for the registered nurse, from primary nurse to case manager. The nurses on the General Medical Unit have adapted well to the new role, and are looking for other changes which might benefit patient care—and them.

Katie currently makes patient care assignments; however, this function will soon be assumed by the staff. Kerry, Lee, and Jane approach Katie with an idea for changing the way patient care assignments are made. They read an article about making patient care assignments by the geographic location of the rooms rather than the current method of matching the strengths of nurses to the needs of the patients, and they would like to implement that model on this unit.

Katie read the article, too. It was a model used in long-term care, and Katie doesn't think it will work in this fast-paced unit. Katie wants to support her staff, so she says, "I'm not sure that model will work here. However, I'm willing to support a 6-month trial period *with the provision* that you read five more articles that address patient care assignments, and if you are still sold on this model, I'll

MYTH O'LOGIC HEALTHCARE CENTER Concluded

help you develop a proposal, then *you* must sell the rest of the staff. Deal?"

Kerry, Lee, and Jane proceed, read the articles, develop a proposal, sell the staff with their enthusiasm (and proposal), and the program is implemented. Four months into the six-month pilot period they ask to cancel the program. They have concluded that this is a model that does not transfer well to the high-turnover acute-care setting.

Analysis   In order for staff to participate, (1) they must possess the knowledge, ability, and skills necessary to the task; (2) they must be motivated to try, within a trusting environment; and, (3) they must have boundaries. Does this case study reflect these three elements?

What did Kerry, Lee, and Jane learn?

1. They can trust Katie.
2. Katie will encourage a new way of thinking, *even when she doesn't completely agree with it.*
3. Katie will provide education and support to thoroughly investigate the new way of thinking.
4. Katie will allow staff the adult privilege of learning (within well-defined boundaries) for themselves rather than being lectured and preached to.

What did Katie gain?

1. Katie now has at least three people on her staff who will follow her to the end of the flat earth and jump over the edge with her—*loyalty* that could not be purchased with all the tea in China.
2. Katie now has at least three people on her staff who will not allow criticism of the current method of patient care assignments—because they had a fair chance to try it *their way.*
3. Katie has set the stage for other innovative ideas. She now has a staff composed of persons who are eager and willing to try something new.

All of these things happened because Katie supported her staff. She provided the education and training they needed, a safe environment within which they could test their knowledge and skills, and boundaries within which they were free to experiment. A true win-win-win situation.

I said win-win-win because the patients win, too. A staff composed of persons who feel good about what they are doing and feel free to innovate, within boundaries, is going to be providing superior patient care.

*June Bowman, M.S.N., R.N. really believes in empowering others to make decisions. When I asked her to describe for me how she went about empowering others, she replied:

> One way is to use the working meetings to try to introduce some principles and values relevant to decision making. I want them to know that I want *them* [italics mine] to make the decisions. I am there to support them. I might let them sink, but I won't let them drown.
>
> Sometimes I think we have to give people enough leeway in their decision making for them to realize that some of the decisions they're making are not going to work. If I'm constantly coming behind them saying, "This is not going to work. This is not going to work. This is not going to work," then I think that they're not empowered and they are not going to try. They are going to turn to me to make every decision and that's not what I want.
>
> First of all I don't think that I have the experience or the knowledge to make every decision. I guess one of my deeply ingrained values is that people don't do dumb things on purpose; that they will rise to the occasion if I give them enough support and leeway to do it; and, that they will make better decisions at the lower levels than I can make at the top level.
>
> I think that if we look at organizations that have gotten in trouble, a lot of the trouble was caused because too many decisions were made at the top and they had no idea what was actually going on at the entry level.

That's a pretty strong testimony to the benefits of supporting others in their decision-making efforts. And, spoken by a nurse who has achieved remarkable success in her field.

───────

The staff member has now demonstrated competency at decision making, gleaned through learning, practice, trial and error.

Only now is that person ready for independent or interdependent decision making; for true delegation, to function in an interdependent role.

Our model now has a third, completed level that looks like this.

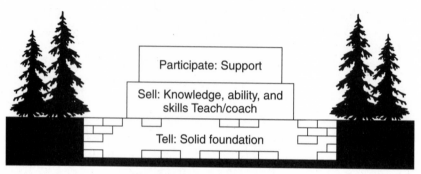

Participate: Support

Sell: Knowledge, ability, and skills Teach/coach

Tell: Solid foundation

Putting It into Practice

LEVEL FOUR
DELEGATE
My Role: Be a Resource

We have now reached our goal . . . true empowerment. The staff member is now in a position to assume total accountability for one or more tasks, given the needed resources and within established boundaries. We have articulated the vision; described completely our expectations; observed an agreement with the mission, values, goals, and objectives of the organization; provided education and training when and where needed; and provided a safe and trusting atmosphere within which to test her knowledge, ability, and skills. We must now look within ourselves and answer a very fundamental question.

Why Should We Delegate?

First, let's look at the plus side of delegation: What's in it for us? If we delegate:

- We'll spend less time *responding* and more time *planning*. (It's hard to live our professional lives running from crisis to crisis as if we were chickens with our heads cut off.)
- We'll be able to sleep at night because our staff are truly *accountable for their own actions*. (We'll no longer have to worry about trivial details.)
- Our staff will have an increased sense of achievement because they will be able to see and feel their importance to the organization's mission, goals, and objectives. (Remember that our main responsibility is to develop interdependent staff.)

When we delegate we truly *turn loose*. Whatever the nature of the task or assignment, it no longer belongs to us. *It belongs to the other person.* It is only when the other person feels the full weight of accountability that we can expect a pursuit of excellence, a commitment to quality, a true devotion to duty.

That sounds so great and so desirable that it's difficult to see the downside of delegation as a management practice.

> Some people still don't get it: In order to get power you must first give it away.

Reasons Not to Delegate

For the sake of the discussion, let's look at barriers to delegation, some of which were described very succinctly by Dr. Frank F. Huppe (*Successful Delegation*. Hawthorne, NJ: Career Press, 1994).

A sense that we can do it better. Actually, this might be true in the short run, and as long as we continue to do "it" and the 3,000 other "its" that accompany "it," we'll continue adding "its" to our list of responsibilities until we finally burn out (dumb decision).

I'm not sure that my staff are ready for this. They might not be. Time to go back to *participate* and encourage them to practice, or to *sell* and teach or coach them.

It takes longer to delegate than to do it myself. This, too, may be true in the short run. There is probably a learning curve here, just as there is with every new task. It may well even *seem* to take longer for us to structure the delegation when we first begin because we will have to keep the steps in the delegation process at a conscious level for a while—only until it becomes second nature. And, since our staff are not skilled at this, no doubt they will be slower than if we did it ourselves. When we are more skilled, both at delegating and at accepting delegation, then we will be able to see the time-saving quality of delegation. In addition, we'll see staff who like that sense of power and achievement and will want to take on more responsibility!

If I delegate I'll have to give up power and authority, and will lose control. Yes, we will. That's what delegation is all about. Remember that our task as leaders is to get things done *through other people . . . not to do it ourselves.*

Difficulty in finding staff willing to accept the accountability that accompanies delegation. Again, we overcome this by ensuring that the staff person has had ample experiences to make dumb decisions, has learned from them, and has received meaningful recognition for having done something independently.

How Do We Delegate?

There are some general guidelines that will help to keep us focused during our initial flights into the world of delegation. They are:

- What is the task? (I must be specific.)
- Who is responsible? (Is it one person or a group of people?)
- What is the time period within which the task must be completed? Does the person (or group) agree that the task can be accomplished within the desired time frame?
- Do I have the authority to delegate this particular task? (We cannot delegate that which we do not have.)
- Have I delegated the authority needed to complete the task, or to make the decision? (If the person or group must come to me for approval to take action, then I have not delegated.)

- Am I prepared to provide the resources needed to get the job done?
- Do I clearly understand and accept that while I can delegate *accountability*, the ultimate *responsibility* for the task or decision remains with me?

What to Delegate

A few suggestions on what to delegate:

- *The routine tasks that are so time-consuming.* Are we really the *only* ones who can check the diet sheet for accuracy? The appointment list for predictability of today's workload?
- *Tasks that require specialization.* Do I have someone on staff who is a computer wonk? Great! That person will represent my department on the MIS committee.
- *Assignments that will keep my staff interested and provide a respite from the routine.* Do I have someone who likes numbers? That person or group will be asked to be in charge of developing the budget, or study the cost-effectiveness of a particular procedure or system of patient care delivery.

What Not to Delegate

Some things are better kept to ourselves:

- *Planning and policy making.* The limits within which one *can* make decisions, the boundaries, are defined by policy.
- *Personal, or personnel, issues.* This comes under the heading of *never.* Any issue here would involve violating a confidence.
- *Rituals.* When the manager's presence is seen as a symbolic gesture of caring: funerals, civic events, weddings, groundbreaking ceremonies, and the like.

CASE STUDY

MYTH O'LOGIC HEALTHCARE CENTER: A VERY GOOD DAY

Nancy Miller, nurse manager, is scheduled to attend a two-day seminar on managed care and nursing. She asks Amy Gregory to act in her behalf during her absence. Having discussed the who, what, when, and where of the expectations and available resources, Ms. Miller departs.

Upon her return, Ms. Miller is greeted with a full report of the significant events that occurred during her two-day absence, including the actions Ms. Gregory took and the actual resolution of any problems that arose.

No problems surfaced that Ms. Gregory was unable to resolve, given her knowledge, ability, skills, motivation, practice, and available resources.

Analysis   Later in the day Ms. Miller encounters the vice president for patient care in the hallway and the following exchange takes place:

> *Vice President for Patient Care (laughing):* I know that you were gone for two days. Ms. Gregory did such a good job that we discovered that we don't need you.
>
> *Ms. Miller (smiling):* Isn't she great? That's my goal . . . to work myself out of a job.

CASE STUDY

MYTH O'LOGIC HEALTHCARE CENTER: A DIFFERENT KIND OF DAY

Once again Ms. Miller is to be gone, and Ms. Gregory has agreed to be acting nurse manager.

The day progressed without any incidents of note until about 10:00 AM, at which time Dr. Jackass appeared. (We all know him. While most physicians are great human beings in addition to being competent practitioners, there are a few like Dr. Jackass.) Dr. Jackass, having seen his patient, Mrs. Smith, moves to review the chart

---

MYTH O'LOGIC HEALTHCARE CENTER: A DIFFERENT KIND OF DAY
Concluded

and screams, "Somebody gave Mrs. Smith Prinavil instead of Vevrapamil. Who did that? Where's that nurse? I want her off this unit!"

Ms. Gregory, hearing the commotion, moves swiftly to intervene. She opens the chart and points out to Dr. Jackass, "Look, Dr. Jackass. You changed the order yesterday. Mrs. Smith received exactly what you ordered."

With that, Dr. Jackass roars, "Nobody tells me *I* made a mistake," storms off the nursing unit, and goes straight to the director of medical affairs to complain. He, in turn, seeks an audience with the vice president for patient care.

When Ms. Miller returns to work, Ms. Gregory gives her a full accounting of the incident and informs her that the vice president for patient care is expecting to see her immediately.

Analysis   Ms. Miller, having listened intently to Ms. Gregory's recitation of the incident, uses this as a learning experience. She says, "Given what you know now that you didn't know yesterday, if this same thing happened again, how would you handle it?"

Ms. Gregory, who is her own worst enemy, and has had all night to think about it, responds, "If this same thing happened again I would still open the chart; however, I would allow Dr. Jackass to find for himself his own mistake."

Note: Dr. Jackass will still be furious. However, he is not going to embarrass himself by going to the director of medical affairs. He will also be quite contrite the next few times he encounters Ms. Gregory.

Digression   One of the most phenomenal leaders I have ever had the privilege of watching was the late Paul "Bear" Bryant, coach of the University of Alabama football team. He was a huge man, physically and psychologically. By that I mean that when he appeared on the sidelines or the television screen he was the only person we noticed. His huge presence, his trademark houndstooth check hat, and his deep voice all served to make him a "good interview" following the football game.

When Alabama won a football game, Coach Bryant said, consistently, "The boys played a good game today."

When Alabama lost a football game, Coach Bryant said, consistently, "The coaches and I let the boys down today."

That's Ms. Miller's role with Ms. Gregory. When Ms. Miller meets with the vice president for patient care, her role is to say, "I didn't foresee that this would happen, and I didn't prepare Amy adequately for it. She is now prepared. I accept full responsibility."

I can guarantee that Ms. Gregory will *never* assume this level of leadership again. It's simple. All I have to do is sigh and say, "It's ok. Don't worry about it. I'll take care of it"—and treat her like an incompetent child.

Boundaries

The boundaries are established by the limits of the accountability, the availability of resources, and the responsibilities of the nurse manager.

Decision Making

Within the boundaries established by the nurse manager, the staff person has full authority to make and implement decisions.

———

Where are we now? We have completed the framework within which our staff can learn, practice, and implement interdependent decision making:

> We provided the foundation: the mission, values, beliefs, and attitudes of the organization and of ourselves—*tell.*
>
> We assured that the staff possessed the knowledge, ability, and skills needed in order to participate in interdependent decision-making—*sell.*
>
> We provided opportunities for practicing the needed skills within a safe environment—*participate.*
>
> We "turned loose" and let the other person have (own) that sense of achievement that comes from doing a job well—*delegate.*

Our house with its different levels of organization, expectations, and accountability now looks like this:

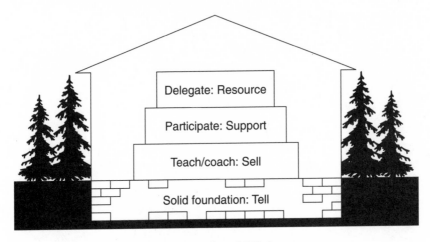

The Completed Vision

The climb to *delegate* was worth it, the sense of accomplishment, achievement, and a feeling of worth and value to the patients *and the organization* contribute to a desire to want to continue to function at this level. And we got there by ascending the levels one at a time—step by step by step. *We can't skip steps.*

A Look at Ourselves

One of our major responsibilities is to take a good, hard look at ourselves, and examine our own natural style of management. I am, by nature, more comfortable delegating than telling another person what to do. Doesn't that sound like Miss Goody Two-Shoes? *It's a terrible thing to do, and I've done it.* There is a basic assumption here that the other person can read my mind and know exactly what I believe, what I want done, how I want it done—all the elements covered in the tell/foundation level. I want to hire very professional, competent people and turn them loose with no guidance other than, "You're a professional—you know what to do." Then, horror of horrors, I call the person in for the 90-day evaluation and criticize her for not doing something I hadn't told her I wanted done. *Terrible! Awful!* And, I've done it.

What this insight tells me is that I must be very careful and make a concerted effort to start at the beginning, and not make any assumptions about the other person's level of functioning. We must go through, together, the four steps.

Those of us who are more controlling, by nature, are going to have to take a deep breath and begin turning loose—one step at a time.

A Look at Our Staff

If we have large enough numbers, consider the levels of functioning of our individual staff members, and plot those levels on a bell curve, the bell curve would probably look something like this:

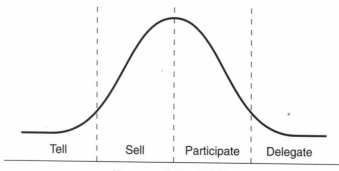

| Tell | Sell | Participate | Delegate |

Expected Staff Mix

As we can see, a few of our staff will be functioning at a very low level; they won't take the initiative and do anything without being told what to do. That's really OK. Most of us have repetitive tasks that need to be done, and we're thankful that we have a few staff persons around who are happy and content doing them. Most of our staff will be in the two middle ranges of functioning, needing knowledge, ability, and skills, or motivation to practice those same skills. And a few will be in the upper ranges of functioning, as in our case study of Amy Gregory, persons to whom we can delegate.

What we want to correct, or avoid, is a staff mix that looks like this:

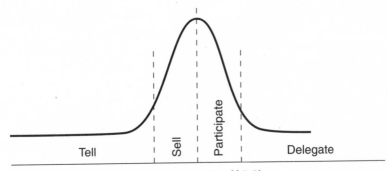

Problematic Staff Mix

When we find, on analysis, that we have a large percentage of our staff functioning at this very dependent, task oriented level we must take action. We are obligated, morally, ethically, and professionally, to provide each of these staff members with an opportunity to acquire the knowledge, ability, and skills needed to function at a higher level and the opportunity to practice those skills in a safe environment. When the staff person(s) chooses not to enhance her job skills, despite all the opportunities, then perhaps she needs to consider a profession other than health care—let her go. Today's and tomorrow's world of health care demands a highly functioning staff. We do her no favor by continually attempting to rescue her. The well-intentioned act of rescuing actually contributes further to her dependency, and *prevents* her growth.

We have applied:

Principle 1: Most people want to live up to our expectations.

Principle 2: Interaction with others is more effective when we meet them where they are rather than where we want them to be.

Principle 3: Given the knowledge, ability, skills, and motivation, people can make their own decisions in matters pertaining to their work.

*Mary Lou Jones, Ph.D., R.N., has been very successful in providing the leadership for implementing this developmental model of management. When I asked her to what she attributed her success, she responded:

It's a journey. It's believing so passionately in what you do that you live it every moment because it's that moment-to-moment building that then results in the effect that you have over time. You deal with the one-on-one, with people in groups, with institutions, with people in communities, and with our nation.

While I've had the honor and privilege of being involved on multiple levels, I still am grounded in the one on one because it is an encounter and it's taking the opportunity.

I try to educate as I go along. I find people where they are and build on that, and help them to grow, and *help them to own that growth* [italics mine]. It's causing them to stretch. It's a creative tension, where people have to do it themselves. It's that internal motivation, but I have to create a climate where that can happen, and *an expectation that they can do it because many times people don't believe themselves that they can do it.*

It's creating the atmosphere and the expectation; communicating and supporting them; and providing the resources for them to do it; and empowering them with the belief that they *can* do it, and that I'm going to support them. And, if they make a mistake, that's OK—that's going to happen. Fear strategies just don't work. We can't give them expectations and then kill them if they don't succeed. They certainly won't try again.

Mary Lou's success speaks to her values and her belief that individuals do have a contribution to make and they *can* do it themselves, with her help, encouragement, support, and adequate resources.

Now let *us* move on and see how we apply this in our day in and day out role of manager.

2

CHAPTER

Applying the Vision in the Real World

Should We Redirect, or Reprimand?

In an ideal world our staff would progress from *tell* to *sell* to *participate* to *delegate* and remain there forever and ever. Sigh—wouldn't that be great? The world that I live in says it doesn't work that way. I mess up occasionally—my staff messes up occasionally. Most of the time we all self-correct (if that is a word). Once in a while I must intervene in behalf of my staff.

There are four values our staff expects us to hold, especially as these values affect our relationship with them. A value is a belief that we hold that is so strong and dear to our hearts that it guides our actions. Our staff wants to know that we *care* about them; they want to know that we are *consistent;* they want to know that we are *fair;* and, they want to know that we are *firm.*

My two options when my staff *does* mess up, whether deliberately or unintentionally, are to (1) *redirect,* or (2) *reprimand.* Of the two, my bias is to use redirection. Not because I'm such a nice person (even though I am), but because it is more effective for most people. It is important that my staff members work with me tomorrow because they *want* to, not because they *have* to. My four essential values are also put to the test within this choice. And, too, consider that if redirection doesn't work I can always reprimand.

In keeping with the principle of meeting people where they are rather than where I want them to be, I'm going to try to come down *one step* from where that person is functioning with the goal of encouraging the person to again function at that higher level. One of the tools I can use to help me ascertain the level of functioning is Maslow's hierarchy of human motivational needs.

I have superimposed Maslow's hierarchy onto Hersey and Blanchard's model of situational leadership because it makes so much sense. Let's look at it:

Delegate — Achievement
Participate — Self-esteem/Recognition
Sell — Belonging/Social acceptance
Tell — Safety and security
Physiologic needs

Marriage of Maslow and Situational Leadership

At the base of Maslow's hierarchy we have *physiological needs.* Isn't that the same as saying the person must have a good foundation, a basic understanding of expectations coupled with good working conditions? When we refer to a good foundation we are talking about the *tell* level in our situational leadership model.

The next step in Maslow's hierarchy is *safety and security.* We talked about the importance of having the knowledge, ability, and skills needed to fulfill the responsibilities of the job. When I have those skills, I feel safe and secure. This correlates with the *sell* level.

Social acceptance also correlates with *sell* because our sense of belonging to the work family adds depth and meaning to our possession of the required knowledge, ability, and skills. It's kind of like knowing that someone cares about me as a person, not just someone who can accomplish a task.

When we talk about *self-esteem* and *recognition*, we're really thinking about someone who is well versed in the expectations, has the knowledge, ability, and skills necessary to accomplish the task(s), and is now out there putting those skills into practice—*participating.*

And, lastly, the person to whom I *delegate* is seeking a sense of *achievement.*

We have already applied this concept. Recall that when Ms. Gregory (who was functioning at the *delegate* level) unintentionally had an adverse experience with Dr. Jackass, we dropped down one level from where where she was functioning, to the *participate* (support) level in an effort to *redirect* her. And, we demonstrated the probable negative effect of *reprimanding* her (with our sigh, and treating her like a child).

Now let's look at a few more brief case studies and see how we apply this concept of more effective to redirect than to reprimand—when possible.

CASE STUDY

> *Gloria H:* Gloria is a nurse with excellent clinical skills who has developed an annoying and destructive pattern of behavior. She has begun to "play up" to the physicians by telling them that *she* knows how they want their patients taken care of, and *she* does it, and they can depend on *her.*

Assessment
Does Gloria understand the rules of conduct (basic expectations)? Is she secure in her position as a nurse? Is she seeking recognition?

Option #1   Reprimand Gloria. Gloria is staff splitting and I have an absolute *thing* about staff splitting! My gut reaction is to call Gloria in and *tell* her to stop (reprimand). I'd like you to look at this next drawing while we discuss why this option will probably not be as effective as we would like it to be.

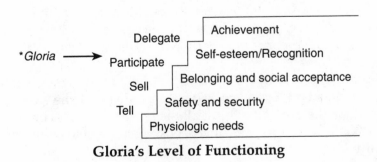

Gloria's Level of Functioning

When we really look at what Gloria is doing, and *why she's doing it*, we can see that she is seeking recognition. We happen to think that the way she's seeking recognition is inappropriate—that, however, does not change the fact that she *is* seeking recognition.

When we reprimand, or chastise Gloria for seeking recognition from the physicians and, further, tell her to stop doing it, we will have done *nothing* to help her get that need for recognition met. That need is still there—*and it will be met.*

While I have the authority to reprimand Gloria, about all my reprimand will accomplish is that: (1) her recognition seeking by physicians will diminish in frequency and will be a little sneakier, and (2) she will continue getting the need for recognition met in another, perhaps less positive way than her current method of choice.

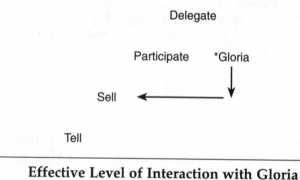

Effective Level of Interaction with Gloria

Option #2   Redirect Gloria. To do that, having acknowledged that what she is seeking is recognition, I must first come to terms with the fact that *her need for recognition will be met, one way or another.* I want to drop down one level and *sell* her on a more effective way of getting those recognition needs met. Rather than my telling Gloria, I want Gloria to tell *me* what motivates her to play up to the physicians. I'm going to call her in for a conference. In this conference I must be prepared to hear what Gloria says, and it might not be what I want to hear.

Gloria might say, "You never tell me I'm doing a good job." Wow! I think I do. Every week at staff meeting I tell the group what a great job they're doing. I put all the cards and letters on the bulletin board for all to see. I even post a staff nurse of the month award.

What Gloria needs to hear is, "Mrs. Johnson said you were just great. You were so patient with her when you took her to the bathroom. She didn't feel rushed at all." Gloria will stand up straighter and walk taller. Is she going to be even *more* patient with Mrs. Johnson now? You bet she is. She might even transfer that patience to another patient.

We expend a tremendous amount of time and effort learning that those of us in management positions must be very specific in our "constructive criticism" with respect to the staff's performance standards. *We must be equally specific with our praise.* Global recognition just doesn't mean much.

We have applied **Principle 2: Interaction with others is more effective when we meet them where they are rather than where we want them to be.**

CASE STUDY

Michael M.: Michael has become a part of Myth O'Logic Healthcare Center's Home Health Agency, having had one year's experience in the acute-care setting. Michael has completed an extensive orientation program during which documentation was emphasized; the "why," the "how," and acceptable standards. In addition, expectations were clearly expressed that emphasized the importance of having the documentation completed in a timely manner.

Upon completion of his 90-day probationary period Michael was counseled about his disregard of the clearly stated documentation policy. He stated at that time that he truly believed that patient care was a priority and that documentation was not, in his opinion, that important. I outlined, as clearly as I could, the importance of documentation to (1) a record of effective patient care (quality), which included what worked and what didn't work for a particular patient (outcome), and (2) reimbursement (cost). While nurses frequently don't like to think about money, the fact is that if we as a company are not reimbursed for our services we can no longer continue to pay nurses to deliver those same essential services to deserving patients.

Despite repeated reminders Michael is consistently late with his documentation and consistently inattentive to the need for complete and accurate information.

Assessment

Does Michael understand the basic expectations of his performance? Does he have the knowledge and skills necessary to provide him with a sense of security in his ability to perform his job? Is he seeking recognition in some form?

Option #1   Reprimand Michael is not complying with documentation policy despite having completed an extensive orientation program, counseling, and repeated reminders. He acknowledges having the knowledge, ability, and skills *(sell)*; therefore, I decide to drop down one step, to the *tell* level. Michael is (deliberately or unintentionally) not meeting basic expectations. Therefore, I have only one choice—to *reprimand*. Michael must understand that I am *firm* about my expectations.

I will restate my expectations in the form of a verbal warning—use of progressive discipline. At the same time, as a condition of continued employment, I will insist on Michael's repeating the orientation program designed to teach the why, how, and standards of documentation to *ensure that he has the knowledge and skills necessary to perform the functions required by his job*. This is also a way of demonstrating that while I am *firm*, I also *care*.

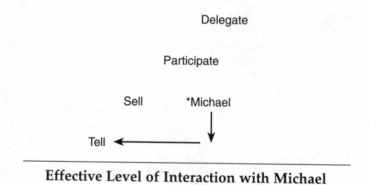

Effective Level of Interaction with Michael

When we examine Michael's actions we can see that his current level of functioning is quite low with respect to documentation. (He might easily be functioning at a much higher level when he is in direct patient care.) In keeping with my options of being able to *redirect* or to *reprimand,* I find that with Michael, I *must reprimand.* At the same time, I can attempt to *redirect* by mandating a repeat of the necessary course of study leading to competency in documentation.

Having done that, if Michael continues to refuse to comply with standards, I must continue with progressive discipline until he understands that I am serious about this. At that point, Michael can choose to abide by policy, or leave—the choice is his.

Option #2   In Michael's case we really don't have another option. We attempted redirection; Michael chose not to be redirected. We redirect when we have a choice; we reprimand when we must.

We have applied **Principle 2: Interaction with others is more effective when we meet them where they are rather than where we want them to be,** and **Principle 3: Given the knowledge, ability, skills, and motivation, people can make their own decisions in matters pertaining to this work.**

CASE STUDY

Michelle R: Michelle is a patient care assistant who provides excellent patient care and has an established reputation and record of dependability. The last few weeks, however, she has been calling in on successive Fridays and Mondays. Sometimes she is sick; sometimes a child or parent is sick. Absences on days that surround the weekend are looked upon far more seriously than random absences during the week. This was thoroughly covered during Michelle's orientation. These absences are not fair to the patients. I know that it isn't fair to the other staff who are there because they have to work harder. Bottom line is, it isn't fair to the patients because the remaining staff must now divide their time among a larger number of patients, thus depriving the patients of the individual time and attention they deserve.

Following the third consecutive weekend of call-ins, the nurse manager calls her into her office for a conference.

Assessment

Does Michelle understand the attendance policy? Does Michelle have the knowledge, ability, and skills to adhere to the policy? Is Michelle motivated to conform to the policy?

Option #1   Reprimand. Based on my belief and my emphasis, I want to inform Michelle that her frequent absences are unacceptable. I want to *reprimand*. Let's look at where Michelle is functioning.

Delegate

Participate   *Michelle

Sell

Tell

Michelle's Level of Functioning

We can assume that Michelle knows the policy and expectations *(tell)* because she has followed the policy in the past.

We can assume that Michelle has the knowledge, ability, and skills to comply with the policy *(sell)* because up to this time she has always been dependable.

We can therefore assume that the issue is one of motivation for Michelle *(participation)*.

This assessment notwithstanding, my gut-level response to repeated absences on Fridays and Mondays is to start progressive discipline. Michelle must know by now how strongly I feel about this and that I am serious about it. Let's look at what can happen when I meet Michelle *where I want her to be rather than where she is* (a direct violation of Principle 2). The interaction might go something like this:

> *(In my office) Me:* Michelle, I've been looking at the time cards for the past month and I see that on each of the last

three weeks we've received a call from you that you can't make it to work on Friday and again on Monday. I know that you know the importance that I attach to dependable attendance, and especially attendance on days that are connected to the weekend. I want you to appreciate the seriousness of this action. This is a verbal warning. You have violated a well-stated and well-defined policy repeatedly. If there is another absence on Friday or Monday, there will be a written warning, then probation, then suspension, then you will be terminated. I want to be sure that I have been heard and understood. What have I just said?

Michelle: You just said I might lose my job. You can't do that to me, Katie. I need my job.

Me: (I'm thinking, Yes, I can, and I will.)

Michelle: Oh, no, Katie. My husband started drinking, you know.

Me: (I'm thinking, No, I didn't know that, but what does that have to do with her absences anyway?)

Michelle: He takes care of the babies for me so I can work. Day care is so expensive. He works three twelve-hour shifts, on Tuesday, Wednesday, and Thursday, and he takes care of the babies on Fridays and Mondays. He gets paid on Thursday night. Lately, he's taken all his money and spent it on liquor, and he stays out carousing after work on Thursday. By the time he gets home—early on Friday morning—he's just so drunk. You don't want me to leave my babies with a drunk man, do you?

Me: (I'm thinking, Oh, that's just awful. I didn't know that.)

Michelle: And, he's spending all his money on liquor. I'm the only one bringing in money for milk and food for my babies. I need my job. You don't want to take milk out of the mouths of my babies, do you? It isn't my fault. Don't punish my babies.

Me: (I'm thinking, I wish I had found this out to begin with. This is terrible. I wonder how I can help? I immediately back up. I started out at *tell* and *reprimand* and now I back up to *sell* in a belated attempt at *redirection*.) Michelle, this is an awful situation to be in. I want you to see Steve Cole in Human Resources—he can be a tremendous help to you;

here's his phone number. And, I want you to call Andrea Benjamin, the local representative for Al-Anon. It's a great organization and they can provide support for you. Here is her phone number.

And, I can give you two weeks to find a stable baby sitter. If there is an absence beyond that second week we will have to implement progressive discipline. The patients are entitled to consistent care.

Now, let's look at what we did.

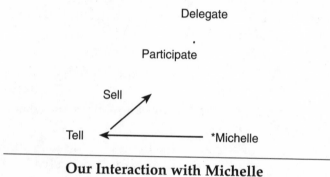

Delegate

Participate

Sell

Tell   *Michelle

Our Interaction with Michelle

We started at *reprimand* and backed up to *redirect*. Our staff wants us to be *caring, consistent, fair,* and *firm*. While we did *care,* we did it inappropriately. We have immediately violated *consistent* and *firm*. Another problem is that we are now seen as being easily manipulated. Michelle is likely to go tell Brenda, Agnes, and anyone else she can find that if I call them in to begin progressive discipline for any reason, all they have to do is to give me a sad story and I'll change my mind—back off.

Michelle, in this scenario, will no doubt be absent on the third week just to test my commitment to *firmness*. Having backed up once, I now *must* have firm resolve and issue a verbal warning.

How much more effective to have started *where she was rather than where I wanted her to be*. Recall that in our assessment we decided that the problem in attendance was likely related to motivation—and it is new behavior.

We then begin the interaction with Option #2: Redirect.

Me: Michelle, I've been looking at the time cards for the last month and see that we have received call-ins for three of those four Fridays and Mondays. I also recognize and appreciate that I have always been able to depend on you. I want to know what has happened to change that dependability?

Michelle: Oh, Katie, I don't know what you must think of me. I want to be here. It's just that my husband baby-sits on Fridays and Mondays and lately he's started drinking real bad . . . etc.

Let's look at *this* diagram for effectiveness:

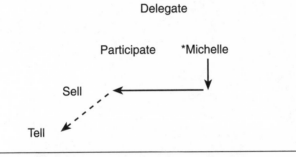

Effective Interaction with Michelle

We start one level below where Michelle is functioning. We listen to the entire problem, offer solutions and help for Michelle to be able to enhance her ability to get to work on Fridays and Mondays, and provide a time frame within which Michelle must make arrangements. We have demonstrated that we *care,* we are *fair,* and we are *firm* in our expectations.

Two thoughts:

1. I must not give Michelle any more help, or time, than I am willing to give to any other staff for comparable circumstances.

2. If Michelle is absent the third week I *must* implement progressive discipline, regardless of the sad story I hear about people not returning phone calls, or whatever other excuse is offered.

It is much easier, and far more effective, to start as high as we reasonably can on this scale of functioning. We can always come down. It's very difficult to go back up.

A final thought on starting as high as we can, given the circumstances. It provides us with what I like to call "wiggle room." We have room to negotiate. When we begin with reprimand, we have effectively backed ourselves into a corner. Where do we go from there?

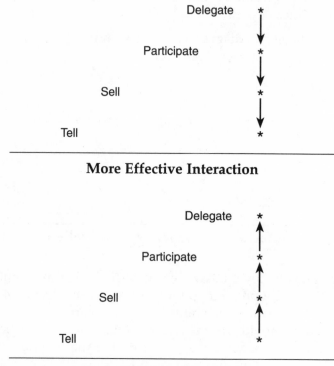

More Effective Interaction

Less Effective Interaction

We've had a good look at the application of situational leadership when our intervention is needed by staff in order for them to function at their highest possible level. We ignore self-correcting situations, we redirect or reprimand when needed and when appropriate, and we do it *now*, not later.

Let's move on and get serious about motivation.

3

CHAPTER

Motivation 201

Or, How Do I Get Them to Do What I Need to Have Done Because They Want to?

We are now ready to tackle that elusive concept known as *motivation*. Do we motivate others? Do they motivate themselves? In fact, can we motivate anyone? What is motivation, anyway?

Motivation, very simply put, answers the question "Why?" about any decision we make, any action we take, any belief we hold.

HOW DID WE GET HERE . . . AND WHERE ARE WE?

During the 1940s and 1950s the dominant school of management said that people were no damn good, they couldn't be motivated, they didn't like work because work wasn't meaningful, and they wouldn't do what needed to be done if we didn't tell 'em what to do. We called this *Theory X*. The 1960s saw the rise of the humanists. Maslow was one of the humanists, along with Carl Rogers, Viktor Frankl, and many others. The humanists' message was that everyone was basically good, work was meaningful, and all people would be motivated to rise to the top, like heavy cream to the top of skim milk, if only we provided the right environment. Remember the "nature versus nurture" controversy? Anyway, we labeled the humanists' belief *Theory Y*.

Who could argue with such a beautiful belief system? *Everybody is basically good!* Well, a lot of us bought it. I said "us." I was one of the people who truly wanted to believe that all I had to do was to provide the right environment, and all involved would eagerly seek to contribute to the common good, would want to do "the right thing." It was such a warm fuzzy way of looking at the world—perfectly in keeping with the tenor of the times, which was "Make love, not war." And, we had Maslow's hierarchy of human motivational needs to provide guidance to us as to just exactly where in the environment we needed to concentrate our efforts. We are all familiar with Maslow.

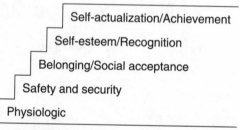

Maslow's Hierarchy of Human Motivational Needs

Maslow's was a theory of deficits. That is, if all (or most) of our physiological needs have *not* been met, our efforts will be devoted to meeting those needs before we can move on to a higher order need. When we consider that physiological needs correlate nicely with our need for a firm foundation in the workplace, it begins to make sense. To carry through with Maslow's theory: If our needs for safety and security and our sense of belonging to the work family are met, then we will devote ourselves to getting our need for a positive self-esteem, or recognition, met. Only now are we ready to seek self-actualization, or a sense of achievement. While Maslow cautioned us not to be absolutist about his theory, we came to understand and to accept as truth that there was a ladderlike quality to the whole concept of motivation, beginning with physiological needs and culminating with self-actualization.

Theory Y believers said that work itself is motivating, and that we will function at our highest possible level *if the working conditions are satisfactory.* We can see that inherent in this theory is that the responsibility for a highly productive staff resides with us as the managers—staff members share no responsibility other than responding to the environment we have created.

Finally, an enlightened voice emerged from the wilderness— one that saw the world and its inhabitants the way they really were, rather than the way we wanted them to be. His name was Frederick Herzberg (*Work and the Nature of Man*. Cleveland: World Publishing, 1966). Herzberg took issue with the common perceptions of Maslow's theory of human motivational needs. He said that all needs are not motivational— some are simply satisfiers. This doesn't negate the importance of the hierarchy, it just puts it a little more into perspective. It also provided some needed relief for those of us who were knocking ourselves out to provide the good working conditions, only to see that a good vision of what we were about and what we were trying to accomplish, coupled with good working conditions alone, was not enough. Productivity was still flat.

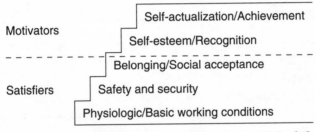

Integration of Maslow's and Herzberg's Models

THE SATISFIERS, OR *DISSATISFIERS*

Let's spend a few minutes looking at and thinking about the integration of Herzberg's ideas into Maslow's theory. Look at the dotted line. Herzberg said that the motivational needs that appear *below* the dotted line are not really motivators—they are satisfiers. In fact, if those basic needs are *not* met, then we are *dissatisfied*. We can half kill ourselves trying to motivate staff, but if in fact they are dissatisfied with their basic working conditions, they simply *are not going to be motivated to function at a higher level;* for example, to make decisions interdependently rather than waiting to be told what to do.

What is included in the dissatisfiers? We can correlate the

need for a strong foundation with our basic physiological needs. We can correlate the need for knowledge, ability, and skills with our need for safety and security. And, we can correlate the need for a positive interpersonal environment with our need for belonging.

Money is a satisfier—or a dissatisfier if there is a perceived lack of adequate compensation for the amount of knowledge, ability, skills, and effort required by the job. If I were to ask for a show of hands for how many had turned down offers of more money to leave one place of employment for another, I'm convinced the number of raised hands would be significant. (Do I really need to point out that if we were working only for the money we wouldn't be in nursing?!) If I had the power, authority, and money to grant us and all of our staff a 100 percent across-the-board increase in salary *tomorrow*, the level of productivity would not increase by even a fraction of 1 percent on a sustained basis.

If it isn't basic working conditions and it isn't money, how do we motivate others?

THE MOTIVATORS

I am probably the luckiest person in the whole world. I have twin grandsons, age 13. They come to my house every other Sunday, spend the afternoon with us, and eat dinner with us. Does anyone else cook for teenage boys? They are such fun to cook for—they're great! They eat everything I can possibly think of to cook, and frequently come back for seconds—and thirds!

One Sunday a couple of years ago our plans were to eat on the patio (a fancy way of saying "just outside the back door"). I prepared their plates and placed them on trays (you know, those inexpensive bamboo trays we get from one of our favorite mall stores). On this particular day deviled eggs were a part of the meal. The guys took their trays, went outside, ate, and were back in the kitchen before I had completed serving everyone else. They leaned over intently and said, almost with one voice, "Grandma, those are the most wonderful deviled eggs I've ever tasted in my whole life. How did you make them? Would you teach *me* how to make them? May I have some more? Can we take some home?"

I couldn't respond to one rave review before I got another one. Well! Am I the cook of the world, or what? Do you think I strutted the rest of the day? You bet I did? That's *recognition*.

Do you think they get deviled eggs every time they come to

my house? They get deviled eggs *anytime they want them.* They're going to die of occluded arteries by the time they're 18 because of all the cholesterol in the egg yolks!

I agree with Herzberg. I don't make deviled eggs for my grandsons because of a *deficit* in my need for self-esteem or recognition. I make deviled eggs for them because that specific praise feels *good* and I want more of it.

It's the same with Gloria (Chapter 2). Gloria will now be conscientious about her patience with Mr. Smith when she takes him to the bathroom because that *specific* praise felt good.

We devote a good deal of time and expend a lot of effort in learning to be very specific with the constructive criticisms we have about our staff's performance. It is equally important to be specific about the praise.

It's the difference between having a staff meeting and telling them what a good job they're doing—even citing objective data to support this observation—and telling one person one thing that is good that has made a difference. How do you think I respond when my grandsons tell me that I'm the world's best cook? I say "thank you" and go about my business. While it is nice, the praise is too global to have much meaning. On the other hand, look at my response to the praise I receive for the deviled eggs! (See Notes for recipe.)

The easiest way to develop motivated staff is to very clearly articulate our expectations at the beginning of the relationship and to reward the person, in some fashion, every time we catch her doing something right.

Judy Prater has found this to be true. *Judith B. Prater, B.S.N., R.N., planned, organized, developed, implemented, and now manages the first home-health-based mental health program in Wichita, Kansas. I asked Judy, "Would you tell me, in your own words, what you did and why you think you have been effective in developing your staff so that they work with you the way they do?" She replied,

> I tell them (new staff nurses) what I expect of them. I tell them what it takes to be a good home care nurse. They will be on their own as independent practitioners; just the nurse, the patient, and the doctor. I tell them that if they want someone telling them what to do all the time, if they want someone constantly looking over their shoulders, home care is not for them.
>
> Then, I am very free with my praise. I always give credit where

credit is due. When I bring to their attention things which they really shouldn't do I never condemn them. I talk about options for improvement in ways that point out how something could be done better—to save them time, or to improve on accuracy. I always try to mention their strong points and to build on their strengths.

They know from experience that I'm very supportive of them, and that I will go to bat for them. I trust their judgment—some more than others. They know that they can rely on me to teach them whatever they feel weak in. They know that I am approachable. They know that I will never fly off the handle with them without receiving input from them. And, they know that I am fair and that I can be trusted.

Analysis Judy Prater applies motivational theory within the framework of situational leadership. She very clearly states her expectations *(tell)*; she teaches and coaches when necessary *(sell)*; she is generous with her praise, giving credit where credit is due *(participate)*, and she expects and rewards independent decision-making *(delegate)*.

Judy also redirects behavior by minimizing weaknesses and building on the strengths of her staff. To quote Judy again,

> I've never had a minute's trouble. I've just been lucky down through the years to have hired some really good nurses.

I think that Judy is being generous with her praise. Read on.

SELF-ACTUALIZATION, OR ACHIEVEMENT

I returned to school when the youngest of my sons was 12 years old, so I frequently refer to myself as a middle-aged retread. When I was an undergraduate I had one professor who took himself very seriously. During one class period he showed a film designed to illustrate Maslow's hierarchy of human motivational needs. The last segment focused on self-actualization.

The single actress in the film was a young woman, oh, perhaps 18 to 20 years of age. She had long brown hair, straight, parted in the middle and hanging down to her fanny. Her dress was kind of sacky looking, and she was wearing Birkenstock's. Now, this was before every middle-class kid and all the parents in the country caught on to the comfort of these shoes and they became socially acceptable by the masses. Do we have the time frame?

The young woman was out in a field of wildflowers, strolling, with a somewhat dreamy expression on her face. She would stop, bend down, pick some wildflowers, smell them, place them in her other hand, and move on, slowly. She continued this dreaming, strolling, and so on until her hand was completely filled with wildflowers.

The professor said that she was self-actualized, and having attained that lofty state, would remain self-actualized for the rest of her life.

This middle-aged arm shot up so fast it took the serious professor by surprise. He said, "Yes, Mrs. Mott. Did you have a comment?" And I allowed as how I did, indeed, have a comment. I said, "She doesn't look self-actualized to me. She looks to me like she smoked one too many of those funny little cigarettes." Well! He didn't appreciate my sense of humor.

Let's look at self-actualization.

CASE STUDY

MYTH O'LOGIC HEALTHCARE CENTER

Sarah Cook, RN, is director of the emergency department in the Myth O'Logic Healthcare Center, a Level-II trauma center.

Ms. Cook awakens on a particular Tuesday morning with an ill-defined sense of dread. What she really wants to do is to pull the blankies up, cover her head with her pillow, and stay in bed. She is, however, a professional. So, she drags herself out of bed, gets dressed, and goes to the hospital, only to find out why she really wanted to stay in bed.

Out of a day staff of eight RNs, three are out with the flu. The flu epidemic means that we can predict an especially busy day with a large number of elderly people coming in with exacerbations of cardiac and respiratory problems. Then, the phone rings: There has been a bad wreck on the freeway. Truly major trauma cases are being triaged to the Level-I trauma center; however, two serious, but not immediately life-threatening cases are being diverted to Myth O'Logic. Ms. Cook is not sure how she is going to be able to handle the extra load, given her staff shortage.

And, Joint Commission is there and her department is to be surveyed this afternoon.

A desperate call for ACLS-certified nurses goes unheeded—remember the flu epidemic? Everyone is short of nurses.

Ms. Cook gathers her staff together and advises them of the events of the day, so far, and what they can expect to happen for the

MYTH O'LOGIC HEALTHCARE CENTER Concluded

rest of the day. The staff—physicians, nurses, interns, unit clerks, registration clerks, and all others present tell her not to worry, they can handle it. And, for the remainder of the day we find those who vowed they would never cross-train happily doing whatever it takes to make it through the day.

The surveyer appears in the afternoon, and Ms. Cook greets him, hands to him the books, and says, "I'm in trauma room 2. I'll be with you as soon as I can."

Upon her return to the surveyer, Ms. Cook is advised that he has found a few nitpicky things (their whole meaning and purpose is life revolves around nitpicky things). There is absolutely nothing of substance to cite as lack of compliance to one or more standards. Further, he tells her that he is aware of the difficulties with staffing *and* the increased demands placed on the remaining staff. *And,* he observed how the entire staff pulled together to get through the day. *And,* that the staff did that for her. *And* that this was a testimony to her leadership—*and* that he doesn't see leadership of that caliber as often as he'd like to—*and* that he wanted her to know that *her* leadership was recognized and would be so noted in his report.

Analysis and Discussion

Well! Does Ms. Cook suddenly grow to be 10 feet tall? Does her head get big? Does she go home and bore her husband or significant other to death with telling and retelling the events of the day? We can bet our bottom dollar that all of these things occur! That mouth is going to go a mile a minute—she is on a roll—a high!

That's self-actualization! A peak experience. And, to emphasize the "peak," she's going to come down off that high—she's going to "crash." In fact, she'll say that she's exhausted and that she hopes she doesn't have another day like that soon because her body couldn't take it. She's right. Our bodies don't know the difference between Selye's fight-or-flight response and self-actualization. A peak experience is very stressful.

Our goal is to recognize specific behaviors that we want to see repeated (remember Gloria—and my deviled eggs). We have a further goal to provide our staff with opportunities to achieve, and to feel that sense of achievement—that they did it themselves. This is what we did with Nancy Miller, who stood in for us as nurse manager and had an "uneventful" day (that is, a day in which nothing happened that she couldn't handle all by herself).

I truly believe that the "peak experiences" are rare and unplanned. Besides, our bodies probably couldn't tolerate too many of them. We can and do seek recognition and a sense of achievement—because it feels good!

Additional Thoughts about Motivation

I think maturity must be marked by the diminishing frequency of the absolutes in life—I find that I have fewer and fewer. Here, though, are two of the absolutes that have stood the test of time:

1. All behavior has meaning.
2. There is a payoff for a particular behavior or the person wouldn't be doing it (or, nobody does anything for nothing).

This leads us nicely into . . .

EXPECTANCY THEORY

What we're going to do now is add some depth to what we already know about motivation. We're going to talk about expectancy theory—a theory developed by V. H. Vroom (*Some Personality Determinants of the Effects of Participation*. Englewood Cliffs, NJ: Prentice-Hall, 1960). Vroom really addressed my second absolute when he said that for any *reward* we seek we must put forth some *effort;* and we will consider the reward and the effort within the context of our *expectation* (or chance) of getting the reward.

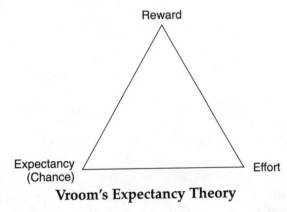

Vroom's Expectancy Theory

Let's pursue this further. The clearest example I can think of to illustrate expectancy theory is Publishers' Clearinghouse. I consistently enter every contest.

What is the reward? On Superbowl Sunday it's something like $10 to $20 million. Now, I don't know about you, but that's a lot of money to me. In fact, on Superbowl Sunday I can be counted on to remain nicely dressed, with neatly combed hair and fresh makeup throughout the day because I just *know* that the van, balloons, representatives, camera, and check are going to show up at my door—any minute now.

What is the effort? What do I have to do to get the reward? I have to take a few stickies off a piece of paper, put them on another piece of paper, put the paper in a stamped envelope, and mail it. Not much effort, is it, given the size of the reward?

Given that the reward is so big, and the effort required is so small, what is my chance (Expectancy) of winning? They are now required by law to tell us, and if we look in the small print we'll find that our chances of winning the first prize are dependent on the number of entries received (probably something like one in several million). That small chance does not stop me, however, because the size of the reward makes that little bit of effort worth it. I'll keep entering as long as I remain on their mailing list. Superbowl Sunday is one day you can count on my being home all afternoon—just in case.

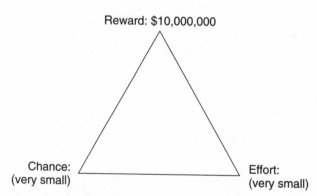

Hypothetical Award Program

Once in a while we hear ourselves saying (usually to ourselves, silently), "Naw, it isn't worth it." We were applying expectancy theory—we just didn't have a name for it.

Last year my dad was seriously injured and hospitalized in another city. I went to be with him—an action we all want to be able to take. My sisters like to be at the hospital during the daytime and I prefer night duty—a system that works well for us. Everywhere I go I listen to nurses because (1) I *like* nurses, and (2) I care about the profession. Anyway, one of my dad's nurses had a pin on that said "Clinical Nurse II." I said, "Oh, you have a clinical laddering program." She said, "Yes, we do." "How many levels?" "Three." "When are you going for three?" "I'm not," she said, and I listened closely as she told me why she was not going to apply for advancement to Clinical Nurse III. (Remember that motivation answers the question why.)

C A S E   S T U D Y

EXPECTANCY THEORY

"I could make clinical nurse III if I wanted to." She identified her chance of getting the classification (the reward) as 100 percent. "I have the education, experience, and clinical skills. I can do the written work, and I don't mind having anyone observe my clinical competence" (a description of the effort). "I'm not going to apply for advancement to Clinical Nurse III because we are required to work mandatory overtime, and we are paid time and a half for this overtime. If I advance to Clinical Nurse III I will assume a staff position and will no longer be on the clock. I will *still* be expected to work mandatory overtime. Even though there is a pay increase that accompanies the advanced status (reward—recognition) it isn't enough to compensate for the money I'll lose by giving up the time and a half at my present pay scale. *It isn't worth it.*"

Discussion My dad's night nurse very accurately described the thought process that led her to the decision *not* to advance to Clinical Nurse III at this time. That thought process was true to form for the integration of Maslow's hierarchy of human motivational needs with expectancy theory. She very carefully weighed the value of the reward (to her); the amount of effort it was going to take to get the reward; and her expectancy (chance) of getting the

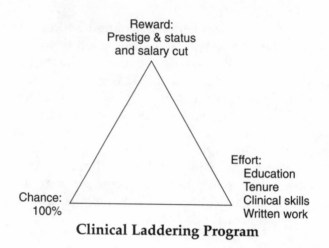

Clinical Laddering Program

reward, given the effort. While money is not a motivator, it *is* a satisfier, and the amount must be sufficient before we can expect the person to seek the reward.

What does this have to do with day-to-day management and leadership?

Everything!

When we want our staff to function at a higher level (making interdependent decisions rather than coming to us for decision making, for example), they are going to weigh, "What's in it for me? (reward), What am I going to have to do? (effort), And, is it worth it?" (expectancy/chance). Our job is to observe our staff, individually and collectively, and to make professional judgments and distinctions between what is a satisfier and what is a motivator.

Let's look at my deviled eggs again—adding expectancy theory to the motivation for recognition.

My husband doesn't like as much mustard in his deviled eggs as the guys do in theirs. Therefore, if, in my judgment, the more important recognition (reward) is from my husband, I will soft-pedal the mustard (effort). In this case I am guaranteed (expectancy) to get praise (reward) from my husband, and equally guaranteed (chance) of not getting the praise (reward) from my grandsons.

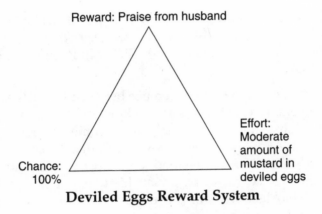

Deviled Eggs Reward System

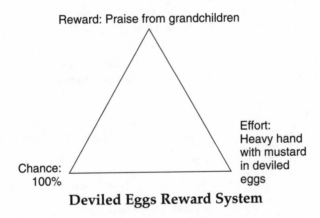

Deviled Eggs Reward System

So, I have one or the other option, and I am in charge. I must choose from which one I want the reward.

Or, do I? This is analogous to having several staff members with different needs. Why can't I put a little bit of mustard in the egg yolks, remove some for my husband, and add a lot more mustard for my grandsons, thus meeting multiple needs? I can, can't I? So, expectancy theory can work with a group with differing needs just as it does with one person.

High Achievers and Low Achievers

- High achievers want to know that they are doing a good job.
- Low achievers want to know how people feel about them. (Hersey, P. and K. Blanchard, *Management of Organizational Behavior,* 6th ed. Englewood Cliffs, NJ: Prentice-Hall, 1992).

OK, we now know the difference between low achievers and high achievers. Low achievers are seeking satisfaction with working conditions—high achievers are seeking recognition and achievement. At an even deeper lever we can see that the motivational needs that we have deemed to be *satisfiers* are controlled by others—they are *external to the person.* (At one time we would have said that the locus of control was external—that is to say that others are responsible for my sense of satisfaction.) The *motivators* are *internal to the person.* (Internal locus of control—I have control over my life.)

Now, there has to be some meaning to this babbling other than my desire to provide a satisfying work environment and an understanding of the importance of deviled eggs. There is. *We can we quantify the difference between working for satisfiers and working for motivators.*

Motivators Productivity = 80–90%	Delegate	Self-actualization and achievement
	Participate	Self-esteem and recognition
- - - - - - - - - - - - - - - -	- - - - - -	- - - - - - - - - - - - - - - - - -
	Sell	Belonging and social acceptance
Satisfiers Productivity = 20–30%	Tell	Safety and security
		Physiologic/Basic working conditions

Relationship Between Satisfiers, Motivators and Productivity

Those who are working only for the money (or other satisfiers) will demonstrate a level of productivity of 20 to 30 percent.

Those who are working for the sense of accomplishment—recognition and achievement (or the motivators), will demonstrate a level of productivity of 80 to 90 percent.

I think that is pretty impactful, and worth paying attention to.

Caution! This is not to be construed as permission to lay people off because look at how much more we could produce if we got rid of the 20 to 30 percenters. We have always hired for an 80 percent prediction of productivity—we just plugged those high achievers into a hierarchical, command-and-control system guaranteed to beat many of them down to the 20 to 30 percent level.

It is also not to be construed as implying that we must work harder. We are already working as hard as we can, and so is our staff, within the constraints we have placed on them.

Our challenge for today's and tomorrow's world of health care is to *remove the constraints*.

To accomplish that, to increase our collective level of productivity to meet the new standards, we must provide a satisfactory work environment, actively seek opportunities to recognize the performance we desire, and provide opportunities for that internal sense of satisfaction and accomplishment so essential to the high achiever. When we have done that, we have applied:

Principle 2: Given the knowledge, ability, skills, and motivation, people can make their own decision in matters pertaining to their work.

Behavior modification provides us with another way of looking at motivation in general and expectancy theory specifically.

On to the next chapter!

Notes

Katie's Deviled Eggs

1 dozen extra large eggs

Hellman's mayonnaise (start with ⅓ cup)
(Blue Plate mayonnaise west of the Mississippi)

French's mustard (start with two teaspoons)

Salt and pepper to taste (you might not need any salt at all due to the sharpness of the mustard)

Place eggs in a deep pan in enough water to provide about an inch of water above the eggs. Add a small amount of white vinegar to the water to aid in hardening the shells for ease in peeling. Bring the water to the boil. Cover the pan, remove from heat, and allow to sit for 20 minutes. Plunge immediately into ice water to chill.

Shell eggs, cut in half lengthwise, and place whites on plate, and yolks in bowl. (I use a Cuisinart because it makes my life easier.)

Mash or whirr egg yolks. Add mayonnaise until yolks are the consistency you prefer. (We like ours to be kind of fluffy.) Add mustard to taste. (This will depend on the target audience for a range of preference from mild to tart.) Add salt and pepper to taste. (They will need only a dash of salt.)

Using a teaspoon, place a heaping mound of fluffy, flavored yolk in each egg white half.

Be careful. Little hands will want to lick the spoon and you may end up with too many egg whites for the amount of seasoned yolk you have for filling them.

4

Behavior Motivation

In Which We Modify Someone's Behavior

PRINCIPLES AND PRACTICE

Oh, but that we *could* modify someone else's behavior! Actually, the only person whose behavior we can modify is our own. However, let's take a look at the process, incorporate what we know about motivation—especially expectancy theory—and see what happens.

First, a brief review of what we know about behavior modification to ensure that we are all on the same page in the hymnbook.

We are deeply indebted to B. F. Skinner, a psychologist, for his devotion to behavior modification. Skinner's basic premise is that the most effective way to ensure that a particular behavior will be repeated, or will increase in frequency, is to reinforce it, or reward it. And, the most effective way to ensure that a particular behavior will *not* be repeated, or will *decrease* in frequency, is to ignore it. (Remember our two absolutes: All behavior has meaning, and nobody does anything for nothing.)

Skinner was not the first person to discover the principles of behavior modification. He was, however, the one who brought those principles to the forefront of thought, especially in the popular press. His landmark book, *Beyond Freedom and Dignity*, first published in 1971 (New York: Alfred A. Knopf), provided the lay public with an easily understood explanation of this concept. For those of us with a more scientific bent, we can readily access thousands of published papers that support the views of the behaviorists.

What I'd like to do is to present a somewhat hypothetical review of Skinner's schedules of reinforcement.

Skinner was deeply curious, for which we are eternally grateful. He wondered what would happen if he put hungry pigeons in individual cages and fed them periodically, on a schedule. The pigeons had a *need* (they were hungry), and Skinner prepared to meet that need by providing food (perhaps corn). The pigeons didn't have to *do* anything in particular to get the corn—they just had to be in their cages.

Skinner decided, perhaps quite arbitrarily, that the hungry pigeons would get a kernel of corn every five minutes, regardless of what they did. (Note: Please don't quote me—that the pigeons got a piece of corn every five minutes. I truly don't remember if it was five minutes or three minutes or two hours. The important thing is that they got a kernel of corn, a reward, every *X* amount of time, regardless of what they did.) This was a *fixed rate of reinforcement*.

Every 5 minutes = 1 reward (reinforcement)

Every 2 minutes = 1 reward (reinforcement)

Every 4 days   = 1 reward (reinforcement)

Every month   = 1 reward (reinforcement)

Fixed Rate of Reinforcement

What Skinner discovered was that over a period of time the pigeons began to make an association between what they were doing and getting the kernel of corn. He came to this conclusion by repeated observations that the individual and unique behaviors tended to *increase in frequency just before it was time for the corn to drop into the hopper*. Some pigeons were flapping their wings, some were pecking, some were turning around. All the pigeons were doing *something*, though *what* they were doing differed, according to the pigeon. It was as though the pigeons thought they were in control; that they had the power to cause the corn to appear in the hopper. Silly pigeons.

This is not a schedule of reinforcement that is particularly useful to us at a human level, although I can describe how it works.

Example Suppose for a moment that I am the housemother for a group of adolescent girls. One of the rules of the house is that everyone will be in bed between the hours of 10:00 PM and 6:00 AM. To enforce that rule I'll make bed checks every hour. When do you think they get in bed? When do you think they get out of bed? Their being in (or out) of bed has absolutely no influence on my making rounds—I'll be there anyway.

Joint Commission now comes to survey us every three years. When do we begin to see an intense effort exerted to meet JC-AHCO standards? Joint Commission will be there whether we are ready or not.

In other words, like the pigeons, what we were doing had absolutely no bearing on (1) whether or not I made bed checks, or (2) whether or not Joint Commission would appear as scheduled. This schedule of reinforcement does not lead to stable behavioral change—just a predictable swing between no action and lots of action.

Skinner then wondered, if the pigeons *thought* they were in control of whether or not they got the corn (reward), could he construct an experiment in which they actually had to *do* something to get the corn. In other words, the pigeons *would* be in control of getting the reward. What were they to do? Again, perhaps quite arbitrarily, he decided that the pigeons would have to make a complete, 360-degree turn in order to get a piece of corn. So, another group of hungry pigeons, another collection of cages.

It is somewhat difficult, if not downright impossible, to engage a pigeon in meaningful dialogue about our expectation that to get a kernel of corn, the pigeon has to turn around. Skinner did the next best thing: He watched the pigeons carefully and *caught them doing something right*. He shaped their behavior. He did this by establishing a *fixed ratio* of reinforcement: For every effort to turn, the pigeon got a piece of corn. In the beginning, when the pigeon made a 90-degree turn in the right direction, a piece of corn appeared in the hopper (a 1:1 ratio). Having learned to turn 90 degrees, the pigeon was now required to turn 180 degrees, and so on, until the turn met the projected goal of 360 degrees.

1 (desired behavior)   = 1 reward (reinforcement)

2 (desired behaviors) = 1 reward (reinforcement)

3 (desired behaviors) = 1 reward (reinforcement)

Fixed Ratio of Reinforcement

The easiest way to establish a new behavior is to reward the effort every time it happens, even if it is not perfect. This is *shaping.* Having established the behavior through a 1:1 ratio, we can now change the ratio to two or three behaviors for every one reward (2:1 or 3:1 ratios).

All right. We have shaped behavior with a fixed ratio. Skinner then wondered what would happen if he continued the reinforcement (reward) on a *variable ratio.* Using a table of random numbers, he constructed the experiment so that the pigeons would now not be able to predict when they would get the kernel of corn. The ratio might be 1:1, or 7:1, or 4:1. The pigeons did know that they would get the reward; they just didn't know how much effort they were going to have to exert to get it—the amount of effort was no longer predictable.

1 (desired behavior)   = 1 reward (reinforcement)
then
7 (desired behaviors) = 1 reward (reinforcement)
then
3 (desired behaviors) = 1 reward (reinforcement)
etc.

Variable Ratio of Reinforcement

This variable ratio of reinforcement (reward) more closely approximates the human condition. Let's stop and think about that. Do we get a reward *every time* we do something right, or good, or desirable? No. Do we get punished *every time* we make a mistake, or do something wrong? Even though it seems like it sometimes, we really don't. We operate within a variable ratio of reinforcement—positive or negative.

Skinner's next question was, having taught the pigeons to turn around, how do I get them to stop?

The most effective way to *extinguish* behavior is to ignore it (nobody does anything for nothing). For the pigeons this meant withdrawal of the kernel of corn (the reward). What he found was that the pigeons that had been reinforced on a fixed ratio increased their turning around for a relatively short period of time—then gave up and stopped turning.

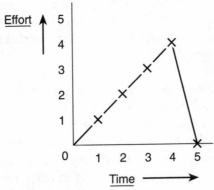

Effect of Withdrawing Fixed Ratio Reinforcement

The pigeons that had progressed to the variable ratio went almost berserk turning and turning and turning. They couldn't figure it out. It had always worked before. If a little effort was not enough, a few more turns and I'll get the corn (Can't you just see their itty-bitty brains hard at work here?) They did eventually give up, but only after considerable time and effort had been devoted to increasing the number of turns.

Punishment works to control behavior. Skinner was opposed to punishment from a philosophical as well as a scientific perspective. As a scientist, his interest was in *extinguishing* behavior, not *controlling* it. His thesis was that if we removed the punishment the behavior would recur. He was right, of course. (Don't you hate it when someone is always right?) Progressive discipline is punishment and is helpful to us in controlling the behavior of those who, for their own reasons, must constantly test the limits, and who also depend on others to help them control themselves. If we removed progressive discipline, we would deprive those individuals of the only dependable controls they have over their own behavior.

For punishment to work it must meet three criteria:

1. It must be *swift*.
2. It must be *sure*.
3. It must be *severe* enough to be meaningful to the person.

In recent memory we can recall the infamous caning case in Singapore. As a woman by herself, I can go for a brisk walk on the streets of Singapore at 10:00 PM and not be fearful of attack. If I *am* assaulted, it is a *sure* thing that my attacker will be picked up, it will happen *swiftly*, and the punishment will be *severe*. I do not have those same assurances in my nice neighborhood, even at 7:00 PM. This is not to advocate caning in the United States; it is to say that if we want punishment to be effective in controlling behavior, the expected punishment must be swift, sure, and severe.

Of these three criteria the most important is *sure*. The perpetrator must *know* that an infraction of the rules will result in swift and severe consequences. With progressive discipline the end result is the loss of a job. *If the job is not important enough to the person to stimulate her to change behavior—let her go!* We don't need people working with us or for us who do not value their jobs.

Now, let's look at a diagram of a few schedules of reinforcement that illustrate what can we reasonably predict will happen if we reward, ignore, or punish behavior.

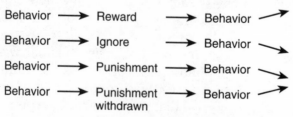

Reinforcement Schedules

Given this review of schedules of reinforcement, how do we incorporate motivation theory, expectancy theory, and behavior modification into a process that will work for us in the real world (as contrasted with a tightly controlled research study)?

The easiest way to modify behavior is to very clearly articulate our expectations at the beginning of the relationship and to reward the person, in some fashion, every time we catch her doing something right.

Most of us, unlike *Judy Prater, whose experience we highlighted in Chapter 2, are not privileged to hire all new staff with whom we can enjoy this relationship. Most of us, as a matter of observation, inherit staff. Sometimes one or more of our inherited staff have drifted off to very maladaptive ways of interacting with others, and they've gotten away with it for a long time because nobody wanted to confront them—confronting them was so unpleasant. And here we are, several managers later and we are asked to resolve this problem that has eluded all our predecessors (who didn't know what to do). *Behavior modification to the rescue!*

*Jean Johnson, M.S.N., R.N., became a believer in the effectiveness of ignoring behavior that we don't want to see repeated, and rewarding behavior that we do want to see repeated, through a personal experience. I asked her to describe it for me:

> I guess the first time it dawned on me that there was something to this was when I had a personal experience with our 15-month-old daughter. I went to a parenting class—that's where you go when they are driving you nuts.
>
> I was complaining about everything she was getting into, and complaining about her constantly trying to get out of her car seat. The speaker said that I was using the wrong approach; that I should wait until she did something right and compliment her on that. So, I did. And, when I complimented her I began to see that she had been motivated to get my attention by doing negative things. I then began to recognize the positive things she was doing. Within a *week* [italics mine] she was no longer trying to get out of her car seat.
>
> I thought, "Well, if it works with kids I'll try it with adults." I started looking for what the staff had done right instead of what they had done wrong, and I began to see real positive results in their work. That's when I realized that people need to see their own potential—they need to see what they are doing right—then they want to do more of it.

Jean Johnson put into practice the basic principles that support behavior modification. She ignored the behavior she did not want to be repeated, and she rewarded the behavior she did want to be repeated. She witnessed remarkable results.

————

Let's look at another situation, one that was brought up in a classroom setting, and in which the entire class participated in resolving. (The names and places have been changed, as have some details, to protect the identities of the persons involved.)

CASE STUDY

MYTH O'LOGIC HEALTHCARE CENTER MEDICAL GROUP

Dana Boone has been employed by the Myth O'Logic Healthcare Center Medical Group for 16 years as a receptionist and as the person responsible for scheduling for a defined group of physicians. In fact, "Dana's doctors" include the original four physicians in a practice that now numbers 21 physicians representing a multitude of specialties.

Times and managed care have changed the world of health care—except for Dana's world. Dana persists in maintaining the same scheduling process she learned 16 years ago. Dana truly believes that physicians should not be able to take an afternoon off—they are obligated to stay and see patients. Patients have learned that Dana will squeeze them in, regardless of the physician's expressed desire to leave the office early because of another responsibility.

The physicians feel a sense of loyalty to Dana; however, they want her to change. The nurse manager has been charged with the responsibility for impressing upon Dana the need to adapt her scheduling routine to the current world's reality.

When the nurse manager attempted to counsel Dana, she simply shrugged and denied that there was a problem.

THE BEHAVIOR MODIFICATION PROCESS

The first thing we must do when we utilize the behavior modification process is: We must *identify the behavior that we want to stop*. Remember when we were learning to chart for psych and we weren't allowed to say that the patient was "belligerent" because "belligerent" was a conclusion? We must be able to specify what we *see* and *hear* that led us to the conclusion that the patient was "belligerent." We must be so specific that if I walked into that office setting I'd know within five minutes who was causing the difficulties with scheduling, denied any problems, and was defensive when confronted because of something I could see or hear this person saying or doing.

What can I see or hear that will lead me to the conclusion that Dana is scheduling patients inappropriately and that she denies that there is a problem? Well, there is a policy about scheduling, and I can check the scheduling for compliance with policy. I can also observe body language for "shrugging," and I can hear, "It's not my problem—the doctors need to stay as long as it takes."

So, my behavior modification process begins to take on a structure and looks like this:

Conclusion: Dana insists on scheduling patients "her way"
                 and denies there is a problem.

Stop: • Scheduling patients outside accepted standards.
                 • Stating, "It's not my problem."
                 Behavior Modification Process

The next step is to remember my two absolutes: All behavior has meaning and nobody does anything for nothing. Dana is getting something out of what she is doing or she wouldn't be doing it. What is she getting out of it? What is the reward?

This class decided that Dana's need for control was being met by what she was doing. That's down there with safety and security, one of Herzberg's satisfiers, isn't it?

Conclusion: Dana insists on scheduling patients "her way"
                 and denies there is a problem.

Stop: • Scheduling patients outside acceptable standards.
                 • Stating, "It's not my problem."

Reward: Control
                 Behavior Modification Process

Now comes the fun part. This is where we're going to apply Expectancy Theory. Look at this circle:

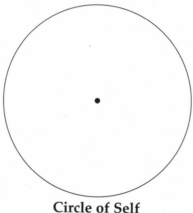

Circle of Self

Everything that Dana has can be wrapped up in this circle. Everything that we have can be wrapped up in this circle. As professionals, we devote a certain amount of ourselves to what we do, and we get a lot out of it.

To illustrate this, I'd like you to put on this hat: You report to me. I delegated to you the task of representing nursing service on a committee. This committee was charged with designing the structure and process for implementing the patient focused care model selected by administration. You did an outstanding job. As a direct result of this decentralized model of patient care, we will now need fewer nurse managers—although the managers we *will* need must be able to develop and manage a flexible and interdependent staff. You feel secure that you will be one of the new managers.

At our next meeting I say, "I really appreciate the work you've done on the committee to restructure for patient focused care—you've represented nursing and me very competently and professionally. As you know, we will need fewer nurse managers as a result of this restructuring. We've looked at our requirements and decided that Shelley can expand her line of authority to also include the area now responsible to you, as well as the ancillaries that will report to her. I wish it could have been different; however, these are tough decisions we have to make. I wish you the best of luck and will be very pleased to provide you with a great recommendation for your next job. Good luck, and if I can be of any help to you, let me know. Thanks again for your superb performance."

As professionals we give a lot of ourselves to what we do—and we are rewarded for that with both recognition and a sense of achievement. We can measure how much we give on this circle. *How much of your circle of self were you willing to devote to what you were doing? That is how much of you I just took away.*

The significance of this is that Dana is willing to exert a certain amount of *effort* (her way of scheduling) to get the *reward* (control). Her *expectancy* right now of getting that reward is pretty good, wouldn't you say?

Let's say that Dana is willing to invest 75 percent of her energy into getting that control need met. This tells me how important that control need is to her. *I cannot change that!* Look at the circle that now illustrates clearly the importance of control to Dana.

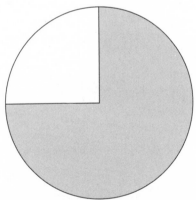

**Amount of Self (Effort) Dana Is Willing to Exert
to Get Reward (Control)**

This brings us to a very important law of physics that is applicable to human behavior: *Nature abhors a vacuum.* We can't take something away without putting another something in its place. (Remember Gloria from Chapter 2? We substituted one form of recognition for another. We were acknowledging this basic law.) Our next step in applying this to the behavior modification process is to come up with a substitute for Dana's expression of her control needs through control of the schedule. We must define what we want her to start doing. And, we must be just as specific as we were when we identified those behaviors that we wanted stopped.

When we truly focus on Dana's strengths we might see that we have a born quality assurance person here. We then think through:

1. Dana is not following the policy for scheduling patient.
2. Dana has a high need for control.
3. We must redefine our expectations of the standards expected with this task.
4. We might assign Dana the responsibility for conducting the quality-assurance audits for compliance with the policy.

Will this give Dana the same sense of control that she now gets by doing it "her" way? We think so. Our plan now looks like this:

Conclusion: Dana insists on scheduling patients "her way" and denies there is a problem.

Stop: • Scheduling patients outside accepted standards
                • Stating, "It's not my problem."

Reward: Control

Importance of control to Dana

Start: Weekly QA audits for compliance c̄ policy

Behavior Modification Process

Does Dana have the knowledge, ability, and skills needed to conduct an audit? Our responsibility is to evaluate her for these skills *before* she is charged with the responsibility of executing them.

We're almost done. Our final step is to bring to a level of awareness Dana's need for *positive reinforcement (reward)* for maintaining the schedule at the predetermined level of compliance with the policy. And to *consistently recognize* her efforts and her accomplishments.

Our completed behavior modification problem-solving process looks like this:

<u>Conclusion:</u>	Dana insists on scheduling patients "her way" and denies there is a problem.
<u>Stop:</u>	• Scheduling patients outside acceptable standards. • Stating, "It's not my problem."
<u>Reward:</u>	Control

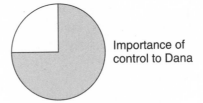

<u>Start:</u>	Weekly QA audits for compliance c̄ policy.
<u>Reinforcement:</u>	• Praise for audits which are within standards. • Ignore "I'm not responsible" comments.

Completed Behavior Modification Process

When I schedule a conference with Dana to discuss her performance, I'm not going to talk about what I *don't* want her to do; I'm going to focus on what I *do* want her to do. This is pure application of what I learned from Skinner: If I want behavior to be repeated I reward it; if I want it to go away I ignore it.

I expended a lot of energy in thinking through what she was doing that was causing grief for the physicians, the reward she was getting for it, and how much of herself she was willing to invest in getting that reward. It was not a wasted effort. I had to think through the problem in an orderly, sequential way to get to where I am now—the problem-resolution phase.

This very focused problem-solving process can also lead us to the conclusion that we have nothing to offer the other person, in which case we must think seriously about letting that person find another source of employment where her needs can be met.

We are at the *sell* level in our leadership grid—attempting to teach, or to sell, to *redirect* a person in a more effective way of behaving within an organization.

The beauty of this model is that once I have presented the opportunity for reward and recognition very clearly—articulated my expectation of her behavior—then I can turn loose. It is entirely up to the other person as to whether or not she wants to go along with the program. Remember, if the other person chooses not to respond to this effort I can always reprimand (punish).

There is evidence that it takes a concerted effort of about three weeks before we begin to see a measurable change in behavior. If we talk to a born-again nonsmoker, we'll find that time frame to hold true. It isn't that the new nonsmoker has "kicked the habit" in three weeks. It's just that it takes that long to get the momentum going. Now the nonsmoker doesn't want to smoke a cigarette because if she did then she would have to start all over again the next time—and it's just that much harder the next time.

Consistency is the name of the game. If we want to establish a new behavior we must be consistent in rewarding it. When we give up and slip back to the old way we have actually reinforced the old behavior with a *variable ratio*. The only thing we will have changed is how much effort she's going to have to exert—how much of her circle of self—to get that need for control met.

Let's look at one more example:

CASE STUDY

MYTH O'LOGIC HEALTHCARE CENTER SKILLED NURSING FACILITY

Barbara Y. was employed as an aide by this SNF when it first opened some 12 years ago. She worked full-time while completing her education and was licensed as a registered nurse four years ago. She is now the day supervisor.

Myth O'Logic Healthcare Center, Inc., would like to keep experienced staff. At the same time the new realities of health care mandate that the role of management must change from one of

MYTH O'LOGIC HEALTHCARE CENTER SKILLED NURSING FACILITY
Concluded

command and control to one of development of a staff that is capable of constantly learning and adapting to new situations.

Barbara Y. is very comfortable in the command-and-control model—it has served her well in her climb to a position of more authority and responsibility. She truly believes that she must control all the actions of her staff or the job will not get done. Further, the job must be done "her way or no way." Barbara's interactions with her staff are very autocratic and abrasive.

When Barbara is counseled about the need to become more accepting of others' imperfections and the need to allow the staff some flexibility (within protocols), she becomes very defensive and hostile, and she changes the subject.

APPLICATION OF THE PROCESS

What is it that I want to *stop* (something I can see or hear)?

1. Changing the subject.
2. Exaggerated body language—rolling eyes, rigid posture.

What is she is getting out of this? Her reward is attention and control.

How important is this attention and control to her (How much effort is she willing to expend to get this attention and control)?

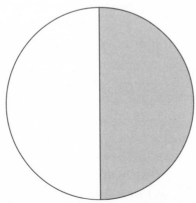

**The Effort Barbara Is Willing to Exert to Get the Reward
of Attention and Control**

What is her current chance *(expectancy)* of getting the *reward* (attention and control), given the amount of *effort* she is willing to exert? (History tells us that it has been 100 percent for several years and through several managers.)

What do I want her to start doing (something I can see or hear)?

1. Stay on the topic during conference discussions.
2. Evidence relaxed body posture.

Does she have the knowledge, ability, and skills to do this? I don't think so, not without some coaching. Therefore, I have an obligation to see to it that she has an opportunity to learn the skills.

Intervention   Send Barbara to a seminar on leadership skills with a heavy emphasis on communications.

Reinforcement

1. Ignore the behavior I want to stop.
2. Reward the behavior I want to start.

Analysis   I will start where Barbara is:

- It is difficult to see the world change so much and hard sometimes to figure out why it had to change.
- The new manager requires skills that most of us didn't learn in school.
- Communication skills have become an essential part of the new manager's role.
- Myth O'Logic Healthcare Center's Skilled Nursing Facility is encouraging all management staff to attend continuing education seminars to update their skills.

When Barbara returns from the seminar, we'll have a conference and I will state very clearly my expectations (stay on topic; relaxed body posture when interacting with others). When Barbara changes the subject or rolls her eyes I will stand still, not say anything, maintain silence, and just look at her until she stops talking and stops the exaggerated body movements. Then I will resume my conversation as if her distracting behavior had never happened.

When Barbara stays on the topic and exhibits relaxed body posture, I'll reward the behavior by continuing the interaction and possibly saying something like, "I like to see strong women who maintain self-control." I can smile. I can also say, "I really enjoy listening to what you have to say, and talking with you." There are any number of ways I can display approval (reward/reinforcement) for her new behavior. I want to reinforce *any effort* Barbara makes toward meeting my expectations—even if the effort was not as great as I had hoped it would be. I want to "catch her doing something right."

Remember that Barbara is in control. She does not have to go along with us. We are attempting to sell/teach/coach her in a more effective way of interacting with others. If she chooses not to participate we can always mandate that she must change. We would rather she choose the new way of her own volition. .

Just a Thought I am constantly amazed at the frequency with which *control* is the major motivator for people whose behavior we would like to see changed. I have to wonder if our traditional command-and-control model of management has contributed to this. And *then* I have to wonder if we just might see profound changes in the behavior of those of us who have high control needs when we implement the new supportive management style. Just a thought.

We have applied:

Principle 1: Most people want to live up to our expectations.

Principle 2: Interaction with others is more effective when we meet them where they are rather than where we want them to be.

Principle 4: We can't change anyone's behavior but our own.

Here is the complete process, or outline, for problem solving within the behavior modification framework. Think about someone who works for or with you. Complete this form just as we did together for Dana and Barbara.

Conclusion:

Stop:

Reward:

Effort:

Start:
   (skills needed?)

Reinforcement:
Behavior Modification Process

GO FOR IT!
It's time to move on and talk about change another way.

5

CHAPTER

Change, Change, Change

In Which We Dissect the Principles and Practice of Change

For the sake of being totally current, and of doing a thorough review, I looked up *change* in several dictionaries and thesauruses. (Is the plural of thesaur*us*, thesaur*i*?) The interesting part of this exercise was that I didn't find *a single* definition or synonym of change that was truly positive, if we consider positive those actions that contribute to predictability, stability, and security.

Change represents a lack of the known, a *lack of structure*. Change can be exciting; it can be necessary; it can be wanted; it is never dull and boring. In fact, just the act of uttering the word out loud is enough to quicken the pulse and raise the blood pressure a bit . . . Selye's "fight-or-flight" response. The knot in my stomach tells me that the bumpy road I must travel to get from "here" to "there" is going to be filled with all the anxieties associated with uncertainty: insecurity, lack of structure, and lack of stability. In other words, it isn't so much the change; it's the journey, the bumps in the road.

Today's world of health care is such that we are in a constant state of change. We barely recover from one, and here it comes again. Our task, as managers and leaders, is to stay out in front of our staff, to lead them through the changes as each one comes along. Even more basic, we must be prepared to lead our staffs through one change after another after another (*ad nauseam*) as the whole healthcare delivery system attempts to redefine itself—to go from point *A* to point *B* when *B* keeps moving. Our goal then is, "When life gives us potholes, make minor bumps."

To make some sense out of a complex subject, I'm going to break it down into pieces:

First: A description of the change process as it affects us personally, complete with a "how-to" guide for getting through it.

Second: A model of an orderly change process within an organization.

Third: Where the models intersect, and what to do about it.

FIRST: THE PERSONAL PROCESS OF CHANGE

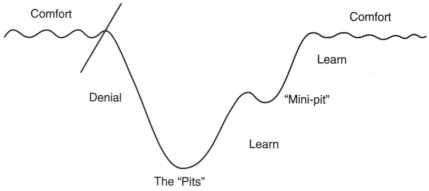

The Personal Process of Change

I like this model of change because it looks "fluid," as if it is moving—and that's what change is: fluid and moving. I sometimes call this model "Katie's EKG of change." I can make several assumptions as I examine this model. Look at that first line, the horizontal one, the one identified as representing a degree of equilibrium, or comfort, or the known, or security. It isn't truly a straight, rigid line; it's a little wavy. However, that waviness is *predictable*. We know the boundaries. Then the change happens, or is announced. Look at the second line, the one going downward. If it's going down it must not be good! (The only line we want to see going down in health care today is one that represents a decline in the frequency of low-birth-weight babies, or catastrophic diseases, or at least costs!)

Our natural reaction to any change is to deny that it has happened, or is going to happen. The degree, or force, or power of that denial, is going to be in *direct proportion to our perception of the threat (represented by the change) to our sense of self* (perfectly normal). Springing forth from this denial, as surely as spring flowers follow a severe winter, is resistance (referred to by Peters and Heifetz as chaos), again in direct proportion to our perception of the threat to our sense of self (and again, perfectly normal). Kubler-Ross's seminal work on death and dying was not really about death and dying; it was a study of our reaction to loss, with the death of a spouse, parent, or child representative of the most profound loss. That's what we're talking about—loss—and we want to be able to minimize the impact of the loss, regardless of what that loss is. The loss might be my job, my perception of the importance of my contribution to patient care, my status within the organization or profession, and so on. In other words, it isn't the actual loss. It is whatever that loss represents to *me.*

The more threatened I am by what the loss represents to me, the harder I'm going to fight to resist the change. I'm going to become very defensive. After all, whatever the perception of the loss is, I don't want to lose anything. Think back to our "circle of self" when we were talking about behavior modification in Chapter 4. It's the same thing—something of importance is going to be taken away from me and I am naturally going to resist.

Even though I may fear leaving the known and entering the unknown, and even though I may mind and resist any effort at change, there is a way to get me to go along with the program, to move from point *A* to point *B*.

HOW TO ACCOMPLISH CHANGE WITH THE LEAST PAIN

The most effective way of accomplishing change is by *decreasing the resistance to change,* diminishing the perception of threat, and acknowledging and tending to the chaos, or resistance. *Slight digression:* An airplane does not fly solely by the force of the engines.

The wings are very carefully shaped to create a decrease in the air pressure above them, thus creating a vacuum into which the plane obligingly rises. After all, many race cars travel as fast or faster than some planes; they still don't fly. That's great for planes; what about humans? OK, let's talk about *us*; how do we counteract the pressure to hang on to the known (like the race car driver hanging on to the ground); how do we "shape the wings" to decrease the resistance so that change can take place as smoothly as possible?

The process of change is complex and requires us to focus on several areas at the same time. The amount of time and attention we devote to each of the areas will depend on our perception of the threat to our ability to be able to function within our environment at our current level of functioning, and with each other as we currently interact (our level of comfort). The anxiety-producing nature of change tells us several things about how to traverse this bumpy road. To overcome the denial and resistance to change, and to facilitate reaching the new level of comfort, we must have, and we must be prepared to provide our staff with:

1. Structure, structure, structure. That structure will include:
   A. Information, information, information
   B. Expectations of their behavior
   C. Attention to their beliefs, attitudes, and values, and
2. Knowledge, ability, and skills to function in the new environment,

We're going to look at each of these pieces and see that they fit neatly and nicely into our model of change.

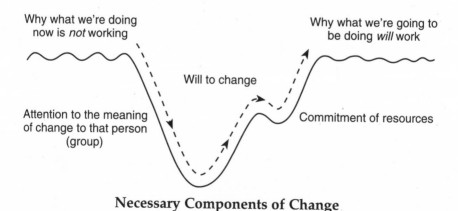

Necessary Components of Change

STRUCTURE

How do I provide a firm foundation so that my staff "can keep their heads when all about them are losing theirs" (to paraphrase the poet, Rudyard Kipling)? I can provide structure through information, information, information. There is no such thing as too much information. I feel so strongly about that I'm going to say it again. *There is no such thing as too much information!* I'm coming back to my natural law: Nature abhors a vacuum. (Isn't it amazing that this same natural law keeps reappearing?)

> I keep six honest
> serving men
> (They taught me all I
> knew);
> Their names are
> What and Why
> and When
> And How and Where
> and Who.
> —Rudyard Kipling

If there is a vacuum, even a *perception* of a vacuum; if information about the proposed (or inevitable) change is withheld, for whatever well-meaning purpose; what can we predict (with a high degree of certainty) will happen? Yep! The grapevine is going to become active. The rumor mill is going to go into full-time production. I don't care how bad the change is going to be, it is never going to be as bad as the rumor mill and the grapevine will make it out to be.

What information do I need? *What? Why? When? How? Where? And Who?*

What

What is going to happen? Is it a complete change within the organization that impacts the mission, or vision? If so, then I must be able to articulate the new mission, or vision. For example:

> Have we been bought out? Are we now a for-profit organization rather than a not-for-profit? What are we about? Are we going to have a completely new management team? Are we part of a chain,

rather than being a sole provider? What is going to be expected of
me? Am I going to have a job? The same job? How is my job going
to change? Will I have a new job description? A new pay grade?
A new schedule? New responsibilities? Am I going to stay in the
same department? In fact, is the department going to continue to
exist? Are we even going to stay open? Are we going to "down-
size"? How much? Are you going to still be my manager? If not,
then who is?

What is it that the person is going to lose, and how meaningful is that loss to that person? Expectancy theory has application
here, too.

Anything that we can think of that will answer the question,
What? And, I think it is safe to say that there is no way that we'll
think of everything. Be prepared, and be honest. If I truly don't
know, I must say, "I don't know. I'll find out and get back to you
by ——." And, I must keep my word.

Earlier, in Chapter 1, I pointed to a study that suggested
(strongly) that, by and large, our staff doesn't trust us. (I'm refer-
ring to the study by Morin, who cited figures as high as 75 percent
for those staff members who don't trust us, or even each other.)
The surest way to validate that mistrust, or to create mistrust
where trust now exists, is to try to make things easier for our staff
by telling a well-meaning lie. Aside from the ethical implications,
there is the cold, hard reality that at some point I'm not going to remember what I said in answer to a particular question if the answer was not the truth. All it takes is one well-meaning lie. And
our staff *will* test us, to be sure that we are consistent (there's that
C word again).

This is essentially the same information that we emphasized
in Chapter 1 with respect to providing our staff with a firm foundation. They must have a firm footing. Otherwise we subject our
staff to slipping and sliding in muddy swamps without even a
compass to tell them they're at least heading in the right direction.
They cannot function at their highest level, even if they have the
knowledge, ability, skills, and motivation, without a firm foundation.

Why?

Why is this happening? For any change to take place, there must be an idea that supports the belief that what we are doing now is not working, and explains also why the new form, function, and structure *will* work. We must be able to articulate this. Why did we sell out to another company? Why are we merging with another physician group? Why has our home health agency sold to a hospital? Why are we implementing product line management? Why are we changing forms again? Why are we adopting patient focused care? Why are we going to use critical paths? Why are we going to use computers at the bedside where the patients can see what we're charting? Why are we going to chart by exception? Why are *we* going to be accountable for the budget? Why are we going to make management decisions? That's your job.

Today's health care environment tells us that all of these changes are directly related to a more efficient delivery system, an increase in the quality of care, and a reduction in costs. A reduction in costs alone, however, is not an acceptable answer for those of us who entered health care because of our interest in helping others. This applies especially to our staff, who have never before cared about or been involved in the budgetary process. (Life was certainly simpler when we operated within a cost-plus budget. Much more expensive, but simpler.) While we acknowledge the need to be competitive, and to change with the rapidly changing demands of

> The information should be meaningful to the individual who is receiving it.
> —Winnie the Pooh (Roger E. Allen)

a consumer economy, we usually grimace and drag our heels when the change is being implemented solely for the purpose of a reduction in costs, without regard to quality of care and outcome.

It is very helpful to include the equilateral triangle of cost, quality, and outcome in any discussion of *why* are we doing this. It is especially helpful to be able to illustrate that excessive costs will inevitably lead to a reduction in quality of care, and that this reduction will no doubt influence the outcome. It is also helpful to be able to illustrate that an increase in quality of care will result in an increase in costs *unless we can devise a more efficient way of organizing and delivering our services.* In other words, change the process.

Balanced Triangle of Effective Healthcare

If we truly believe that we provide a superior service (quality) with good and predictable outcomes, then it stands to reason that we want to continue providing that service. That may mean that in today's world of managed care, integrated delivery systems, and capitation we must change the way we provide that service (critical paths, patient-focused care, self-directed work teams, product line management, etc.), or we must join forces with another organization (physician practice group, hospital, home health agency, rehabilitation facility, hospice, etc.). These are choices that are being made every day in order for us to be able to continue to provide that superior quality of care. If we cannot deliver a quality product for a reasonable cost, as seen in the eyes of today's health care consumer, we will close, or cease to exist. It's that simple. And, if we close, where will patients go to receive the quality of care we know we provide?

When costs exceed the expected outcome and/or quality, or if quality and/or outcome are not consistent with the cost, then there *must* be a change in one of the three components in order to provide a balanced triangle.

How Excessive Costs Affect Quality and Outcomes

At another level it might be . . . why are we changing to "critical paths"? What is wrong with the old paper-and-pencil care plans we are accustomed to using? Again, I must be prepared to justify the change on the basis of the benefit to the patient and the benefit to the staff. I see critical paths, for example, as a great way to stay focused on "our" patient rather than "my" patient, and truly believe that they contribute greatly to increased interdepartmental communications and collaboration with regard to a particular patient. The result of this much improved communication and collaboration is better patient care. *The most important element in this articulation of why we must change is that we must believe it.*

What Are Our Options When We're Faced with Change

If there are changes taking place with which I truly disagree, and I cannot support my disagreement with objective data, then I have a moral, ethical, and professional responsibility to actively investigate and pursue the benefit(s) of the change(s) until I can see that the three elements of cost, quality, and outcome have been addressed to my satisfaction; only then can I be truly supportive of my staff. I cannot fake this belief. If I don't believe it, my body language alone will give me away. My staff will know it and I will have successfully established a distrust that will be hard, if not impossible, to overcome.

A second option I have is to consider the long-range goal. If I believe that this change—whatever its magnitude—is a temporary blip on the way to bigger and better things to come (a not unheard-of occurrence), then my obligation is to take a deep breath, get into a survival mode, and get out there and provide the leadership that a team deserves when it is working its heart out just to make it through the day. I'm going to have to provide a generous supply of "Yes, we can." I must recognize and prepare for a decline in my own level of productivity during a "survival" mode; this will accompany a similar decrease in the productivity level of my staff.

If I cannot in good faith support either option 1 or option 2, then I must select option 3: submit my resignation. I cannot support my staff unless I can first support the mission and vision. I cannot respond positively to my staff's "what?" and "why?" until I have first addressed my own "what?" and "why?"

If I am simply "going along with the program because I need the job," then my level of productivity is going to decline to that lower level we illustrated when we discussed motivation. I am going to be functioning at 20 to 30 percent of my potential. It will be almost impossible to lead and guide my staff through the process of change when I am at such a low level myself. In fact, I don't think it can be done. My staff deserves better than that.

When?

When is this change to take place? If it is to take place all at once, be honest about it. If there is a target date, post the date in a conspicuous place. Include a little leeway; for example, "The new monitors will be up and operational between February 15 and February 28." If it is to be incremental, be honest about it. Diagram the implementation plan. If it is to take place in phases, describe the phases and the anticipated time for completion of each of the phases. If it is a complex change, involving several departments, sometimes a PERT (Performance Evaluation Review Technique) chart is helpful to provide the needed structure.

A PERT chart can be as simple or as complex as our imaginations will allow. I happen to be of the KISS school (Keep It Simple, Stupid), primarily because if it is simple, I am more inclined to pay attention to it, and more inclined to remember it.

PERT charts are also helpful in illustrating the steps to be taken in the process of change, even within one department, because we can identify not only the task to be completed but also

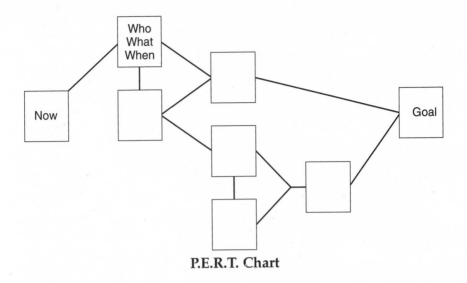

P.E.R.T. Chart

the person responsible for the task and the projected date of completion.

The boxes in the PERT chart can be filled in with Magic Markers, even using different colors for different departments, or functions . . . another way of adding a visual touch to our need for structure.

C A S E   S T U D Y

A large grocery store in my neighborhood recently underwent an expansion from 40,000 square feet to 70,000 square feet, including construction of a two-story parking garage. During this 18-month period of construction and expansion the store remained open all but one day . . . a remarkable achievement.

Several new departments were added to my familiar haunt, many of which I never dreamed would be found in a *grocery store,* for heaven's sake! (A booth for purchasing a *cellular phone* in a *grocery store?!*) I spent 18 months not knowing where the eggs were from one week to the next. (Serious when I consider the demand for deviled eggs at my house!)

CASE STUDY Concluded

Someone, perhaps the contractor, perhaps the store manager, constructed a PERT chart on drafting paper and posted it just inside the old front door of the store, beside the time clock, so the employees couldn't miss it. Nosy customers like me couldn't miss it, either. As the departments, or aisles, or tasks were completed, the PERT chart boxes were filled in with various colors.

It provided a very colorful, visual reminder that progress was being made . . . to the customers as well as the employees, who were undergoing a very stressful transition from neighborhood supermarket to megasupermarket.

How

We must know how we're going to get there. My staff must also know that we have the capability, the resources needed to get to the new level of comfort, however that is defined.

If we need new knowledge, ability, and skills to function in the new order, then I must be prepared to assure my staff that they will have that training. The training can be as varied as cross training, team building, learning to use a new computer program, constructing a zero-based budget, or learning how to participate on a committee (this is a learned skill, too). This is a great place to get staff input. While I probably have a pretty good idea of the kinds of training my staff needs I must invite *them* to tell *me* what *they* perceive their needs to be (it's called meeting them where they are rather than where I want them to be or even think they are). Having done this, it is essential to incorporate some of their identified needs into the training module(s). This is consistent with our earlier discussion of inviting their opinions and requiring objective data in support of their opinions, a continuation of their involvement in the decision-making process.

> Obstacles are those frightful things you see when you take your mind off your goals.
> —Anon

In keeping with my belief that my staff must have information, information, information, I can develop or cause to be developed a training plan that will illustrate who gets trained for what, and when, to post on the bulletin board. A visual reminder of a verbal commitment.

Date	Day	Hour	Class
April 2	Tuesday	1–2 A.M.	Charting by exception
		8–9 A.M.	Charting by exception
		9–10 A.M.	Charting by exception
		1–2 P.M.	Charting by exception
		8–9 P.M.	Charting by exception
April 3	Wednesday	1–2 A.M.	Charting in the computer

etc . . .

Training Schedule

Where

Anticipate the questions related to where *from the perspective of the staff affected by the change!* I must be prepared to answer these questions, for I *will* get them. They are of vital interest to my staff, individually and collectively.

If we are going to have new monitors, where will they go? We don't have room for them without moving equipment (which we see as essential to a smoothly functioning unit). What do you mean replacing the chairs in the rooms with beds for family members? I can't get to the window side of the room now to check on the IV when it's in that arm! Will I have to take the patient to the lab for the new blood work since we won't have lab-based phlebotomists? We're expanding our territory to include what county? You mean I'm going to have to go there?

Are we going to move to another department? Are we going to move within this facility? Are we going to have to go to another building? In another part of town?

Who

> Who is going to be impacted by this change? Is it me? Is it you? Is it my friend in accounting? Is it the patient? Only one group of patients, or all the patients?
>
> Who's in charge? Are you going to be there—are you going to be the rudder on whom I can depend as we go through this? If you're not going to be there, who is? Who knows what's going on around here, for crying out loud. Does *anybody* know?

These are all anxiety producing and add to the instability and insecurity my staff is feeling. Some of the emotional issues this question brings forth include:

> If I have to report to another person, that person doesn't know me, and doesn't know my little quirks, and that I am always at my worst on Tuesday, and always at my best on Thursday; and that when I'm frustrated I get real quiet; and when I'm mad I have to go off alone for a while and think about it before I can deal with it; and, I'm probably the best person in the whole place when it comes to working with the elderly, but I don't do too well with whiners (I'm working on it), and that I am extremely dependable, given my level of ability. For example, I hate numbers. It took me forever (it seemed like) to establish a relationship with you . . . I'm not sure that I have the energy to do it again.

We must know who is impacted and who is in charge! There is enough stress involved in any change without having to wait for a leader to emerge from a vacuum. (The problem with that principle is that it is too true! It's just that the leader who emerges in the vacuum is not always the *best* leader . . . better to be identified out front and prevent that vacuum from occurring).

What have we accomplished? We have just answered the most essential question in all of changedom: *What's in it for me?*

That's called structure! It includes information that answers the question, what's in it for me; expectations of behavior; and attention to beliefs, attitudes, and values during the period of denial and resistance to change. We want to control the angle of descent!

Look at the following diagram on the left side of the page. The steep angle of descent is matched by a steep angle of recovery. *Pay attention to the angle!* Imagine the amount of time and effort required to go up that steep incline to the new level of comfort/equilibrium.

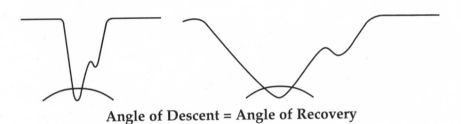

Angle of Descent = Angle of Recovery

Now look at the diagram on the right side of the page. *Pay attention to the angle!* Imagine how much *less* time and effort it is going to take to climb this hill!

Principle: The more sudden and precipitous the change, the longer and more difficult the period of recovery.

There is a very good reason for devoting so much time and effort to this period of denial and resistance. It comes to us straight out of crisis theory, and I'm convinced that the crisis folks stole this one from the physicists: Remember this one from your physics class? *For every action there is an equal and opposite reaction.*

Digression   During the course of a conversation, a pilot sitting next to me in an airport decided to enlighten me with the information that a "safe landing is no more than a controlled crash." While those are not words that a frequent flier wants to hear, they really made an impact on me (another word I'd rather not use in the context of flying). My goal, then, with my staff, when the inevitable change appears, is to "control the crash"; to provide the conditions for a "safe landing."

This tells us very clearly that if we want a relatively smooth transition, we will concentrate our efforts on the period of denial and consistently acknowledge and deal with the chaos (resistance). The transition will not only proceed more smoothly, it will be more cost-effective. It is going to take two to three times as much time, effort, and money to recover from traumatic crash than from a "controlled crash."

*Mary Lou Jones, Ph.D., R.N., recalled a successful change and also shared her view of why the change was successful:

> I was responsible for providing the leadership at Florida Hospital for introducing a clinical management system in the neonatal intensive-care unit. This system included care maps which were based on the developmental age of the baby at the time of birth. It was a process that took two years to see to completion.
>
> We brought in Karen Zander, R.N., from the Center for Case Management, who provided education and consultation for us. We organized teams which functioned as task forces; and we had a multidisciplinary advisory committee which had representation from academicians, clinicians, and administration.
>
> The care maps were thoroughly researched using data from a survey of neonatal services from a multicounty area. They were also tied into ALOS, DRGs, and outcome criteria which included community-based services. We were able to analyze the effectiveness of our care around those outcomes, and that is used today as the performance improvement system that is required by JCACHO. The neonatal core group is a multidisciplinary group that meets monthly to discuss operational issues, clinical issues, the laboratory and management of cultures, respiratory therapy, infection control—a whole host of issues, which also included our interaction with the community.
>
> This system is now being modeled in the rest of the house.
>
> I believe that one of the reasons for this successful change was the methods which were used in program development. There was effective planning and attention given to education prior to implementation.
>
> I think that so often we get in a "quick, hurry up, we need to do this" mode, then the program falls flat on its face because the attention hasn't been given in the right place.
>
> We have garbage in, garbage out.

We have now reached the end of our rope; we're exhausted; we're in "the pits." My major responsibility here is to recognize the level of stress, the degree of disorganization, the lack of ability to pay attention to detail; in fact, the lack of ability to focus on *anything* that requires complex decision-making skills. This is not a time for learning new knowledge, abilities, and skills. We cannot learn when our stress level is this high.

Take a Stress Break

We all have goodies in our "bag of tricks" that we pull out for stress reduction: bitch sessions, pity parties, relaxation exercises, physical activity, and so on. Add another one: Take a break and fold and fly a paper airplane. It is totally foolish. It has absolutely no redeeming social values. It has no purpose. It is simple. It can be mastered in one sitting. In other words, it has all the qualities we want and need to provide a little harmless, productive diversion from the slings and arrows of the real world.

While going through the process of folding and flying a paper airplane, we are actually applying a principle derived from theories of adult learning.

Principle: For learning to take place, the gap between our current knowledge, ability, and skills and our needed (future) knowledge, ability, and skills must not be seen as extreme, or to provoke high anxiety.

Let's revisit our model of change

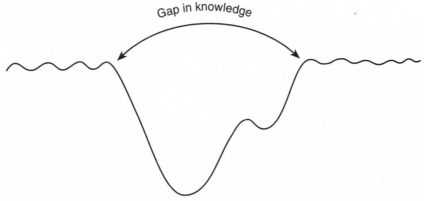

Gap in knowledge

Gap in Knowledge Is Too Great for Learning to Take Place

Look at the gap between where we are now functioning and where we are expected to be functioning within a given period of time.

My efforts at providing structure have been directed toward reducing this gap, counteracting chaos, and reducing anxiety, for the purpose of preparing my staff for the learning that must take place in preparation for the new state of equilibrium.

Now, follow along with me as we fold and fly a paper airplane. (See directions on page 93.)

Even though I may think that I have done a magnificent job of organizing the learning experience and coaching my staff in the simple skill of folding and flying a paper airplane, I'm going to find that quite a few got confused on the third fold. This is a simple exercise, and I have a staff of very bright people. What principle does that confirm for us? *That people under extreme stress are not in a learning mode.* Attempts to initiate grand and glorious learning programs at this time are a waste of time, effort, and money!

Given that I have provided my staff with an opportunity to grieve for what they perceive they will be losing with the prospective change, the structure they must have to prepare for the new, and attention to their level of stress and anxiety, my staff is now ready to embark on their second major task: acquiring the knowledge, ability, and skills necessary to function in the new environment.

KNOWLEDGE, ABILITY, AND SKILLS

New knowledge, ability, and skills means education and training. Let's just design the course, or send them off to a course and be about our business! Not that simple; adults just don't work that way.

We are indebted to Carl Rogers for his contribution to our understanding of the learning process (*Freedom to Learn*, 3d ed. Columbus, OH: Charles E. Merrill, 1994).

Role of the Teacher

Rogers said, essentially, that the teacher, in fact, doesn't really teach. The teacher manipulates or facilitates learning.

If we are pure believers of Skinner's theories of behavior

Folding and Flying a Paper Airplane
start with an 8½" × 11" piece of paper and follow drawings

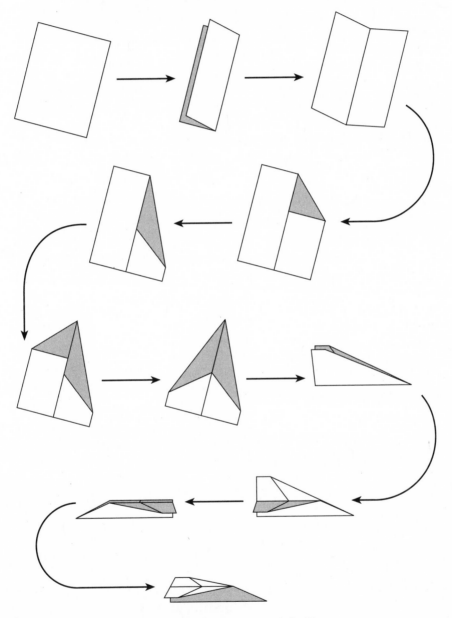

Start your engines and fly!!!

modification, then we will believe that we can "manipulate" behavior with the appropriate schedule of reinforcement. If, however, we believe (as I am sure most of us do) that the other adult is
in control, in charge, and has a choice in this process of learning,
then we will believe that the teacher "facilitates" learning. If the
teacher can "facilitate," then the teacher can also "hinder." My job,
then, is to "facilitate" the learning on the part of my staff so that
they can function at an optimal level in the new environment.

While Rogers discussed numerous principles of learning, we
can extract three and apply them to the process of learning to function within a new structure (whether that means a change in an individual role or for the entire organization). We'll look at the three
collectively, and discuss the implications of them individually.

1. The person will learn what he or she perceives to be
    helpful.
2. Experiences that lead to change in self tend to be resisted.
3. The "self" must be nonthreatened for learning to take
    place.

Now let's return to our model of change.

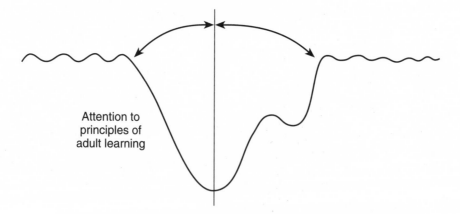

Reducing the Gap in Knowledge to Facilitate Learning

I can see clearly now why I devoted so much time and energy
to my staff during the slippery slope of denial and resistance; I was
actually applying Rogers's first principle. I wanted my staff to see

that being able to function within the new environment would be helpful to them. I also applied principles two and three: I was careful not to say that the *person* had to change—just the *function;* and I assured my staff of a safe environment within which to learn and practice the new skills. (I also applied these same principles within the context of behavior modification).

The Mini-Pit

The climb up to the new level of equilibrium will probably see a slight regression in mood and ability to learn about halfway to the goal. I call this a "mini-pit." I think that it's helpful to expect this regression and to prepare for it.

"Half-Way Party"

Celebrate the fact that we've made it halfway—an acknowledgment of progress, if you will. Provide everyone with half a paper plate, half a sandwich, half a cookie, half a cup of cocoa. Celebrations are common at the halfway point in football games—why not include that halftime celebration within our model of change; a recognition of our efforts and progress in reaching the goal.

THINGS YOUR TEACHER NEVER TOLD YOU

1. Know your material. Haven't we been consistent in saying that we really need to know the answers to the questions *before we ask them?*

2. Begin with where your audience is. In this case we can make an assumption that most of them don't know how to fold and fly a paper airplane.

3. Tell 'em and show 'em what you're going to tell 'em and show 'em. We're going to tell them exactly what we're going to do, and how we're going to do it.

4. Tell 'em. Now we actually do it.

5. Tell 'em what you told 'em. We then review the process; this is how we got from point *A* to point *D*. We repeat ourselves a lot.

6. Accept that, at best, our audience will remember 30 percent of the content.

Application of Principles

We have applied several of our foundational principles during this process of personal change:

Principle 2: Interactions with others is more effective when we meet them where they are rather than where we want them to be.

Change represents a loss to the person, and this is where we began our interactions with our staff: in recognizing the importance of the loss while at the same time acknowledging the need for something new.

Principle 5: Any effort to implement change will be met by a degree of resistance proportional to the meaning of the change to the person.

We emphasized the need to accept what the proposed or actual change represented to the person as the starting place for our interactions; and, we also recognized and expected the resistance to the change (chaos) to persist throughout the change process.

Principle 6: Communication is most effective when the speaker and the audience speak the same language.

We described and reinforced the need for change in the language of benefits to the patient and to the staff, What's In It For Me?

And, we incorporated principles of learning derived from Carl Rogers into our model of personal change.

Having thoroughly dissected the personal process of change, I want to spend a little time looking at organizational change.

SECOND: A MODEL OF ORGANIZATIONAL CHANGE

Planned Organizational Change

Wow, that looks complex! I want to break it down into its component parts and see how they relate to the whole.

Mission Statement
Every organization has a mission statement. It specifies the "why" of the organization's existence. University centers frequently include the concepts of "education, research, and patient care" in their mission statements. This tells us very clearly that these three components are equally important to their purpose in being. For-profit organizations often mention a "return on investment" as a component, in addition to quality patient care. Not-for-profits traditionally cite "service to the community" along with their definition of quality patient care. The mission statement, then, really specifies clearly the organization's purpose in life.

Strategic Plan
The strategic plan is a dynamic (meaning it's flexible) three-to-five-year, market-based plan that describes how the organization should proceed, given the external and internal environments and its resources, in order to fulfill the mission statement. The strategic plan is usually written in generalities; for example, "Enlarge our presence in the high-tech home-care market."

Goals and Objectives
Even if MBO (management by objectives) is not the defining administrative style, the organization still identifies goals and objectives for the fiscal year that must be met in order to fulfill the strategic plan and fulfill the mission statement. Goals and objectives are specific and measurable, such as, "Develop and implement a home-care chemotherapy program for oncology patients within the Myth O'Logic Medical Center's Home Health Agency in FY 19—."

The Process
In this step we put into action the goals and objectives. We define. Who is the customer, the target market? Is it the patient, the physician, the managed care organization?
1. *What* does the customer need that we can provide?
2. *Where* does it need to be done?
3. *How* does it need to be done?

4. *When* does it need to be done?

5. What *standards* must be met

Collectively, these five questions must answer the basic question "Why?" and that Why must state that these actions meet the goals and objectives, which must fit into the strategic plan, which must fulfill the mission statement.

Who

Only now are we ready to say, "Who is the best person (professional, nonlicensed, semiskilled, etc.) to provide this service? Can one person do all of these functions, or do we need to divide the tasks? And, how many 'Who's' will it take to accomplish the goals and objectives—which must fit into the strategic plan." OK, we get the picture!

Organizational Chart

An animal can grow to a length of six inches before it needs a skeleton. Likewise, if we have only a few people working together toward a common goal, and all of the functions can take place in a single location, we don't need an organizational chart. However, when our tasks are many and specialized (nursing, medicine, social work, laboratory, pharmacy, medical imaging, housekeeping, finance, etc.), we do need an organizational chart. The purpose of an organizational chart is to ensure accountability for one or more tasks, and to ensure communications between the specialized areas. The difficulty we have experienced in health care is that we have become so specialized, and so territorial about our specialties, that we have lost sight of the purpose of our existence—the health of the patient. Our organizational charts have begun to resemble the Egyptian pyramids, with layer upon layer of management and administration. The result of this layering has been a decline in the effectiveness of our communications and decisions, an increase in our specialization, and lack of accountability for the total care of the patient.

Today's organizations are attempting to "flatten" this pyramid, to reduce the number of layers, and to demand decision making by first-line managers and also nurses and ancillaries at the patient care level. Accountability is being pushed down to the bedside, whether that bedside is in an acute-care facility, long-term care, home health agency, physician's office, clinic, or other. The ultimate winner will be the patient. Hooray!

Form Follows Function

The orderly process of change within an organization, then, is to proceed from the mission statement to the strategic plan to the goals and objectives to the process (the function) to the person responsible to the organizational chart (the form) to the goals and objectives to the strategic plan to the mission statement.

We get into trouble when we attempt to alter the organizational chart and eliminate positions (the form) without first changing the function. It's the old, "Do more of the same with fewer resources," and it hasn't worked. If we are to have fewer resources, then we must change the process. That doesn't mean that we have to provide a lesser quality of care—it *does* mean that we must function in new and unique ways. Just because we've always done something one particular way doesn't mean we must continue to do it that way. *We must learn to color outside the lines.*

THIRD: INTERSECTION OF PERSONAL AND ORGANIZATIONAL MODELS OF CHANGE

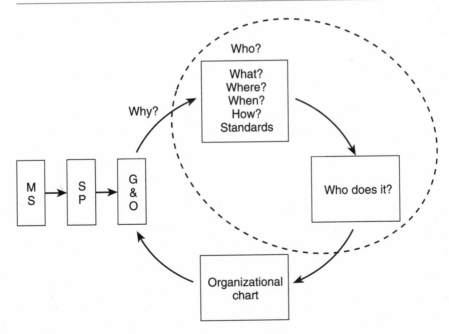

Intersection of Personal and Organizational Models of Change

Our models of change intersect with the process, the designated who, and the provider of the process. A change in any one of these areas will affect one or more of us at a very intimate level, in our guts, in our sense of professional self-worth. These are the emotional bull's-eyes that bring forth denial and chaos.

Analogy We all know that a clean, surgical incision heals better than a dirty, ragged cut. Let's think about that as it compares with a change.

A clean, surgical incision takes place in a surgical suite that is fully prepared *before* the patient is put on the table:

1. The customer, the patient, knows exactly what is going to happen to him or her, when, where, why, and by whom.
2. The entire staff knows what the surgical procedure is going to be.
3. All resources necessary for the surgical procedure are in place.
4. Each member of the staff knows what his or her role is to be, and the importance of that role to the success of the surgery.
5. Each member of the staff has the knowledge, ability, and skills to fulfill his or her role.
6. Each member of the surgical team is totally focused on completing a successful surgery for the customer, the *patient*.
7. Ample time has been allotted for the procedure to be completed.
8. Emergencies are anticipated and prepared for with supplies and protocols.
9. The right number and skill mix of staff are present.
10. Preparations have been made for postoperative care.
11. *Only now does the surgeon make the incision, initiate the change.*

I can anticipate that our surgical patient will recover from this traumatic event and be in better condition because of it. I can also anticipate that the recovery, while fraught with some pain, will be predictable, hopefully uneventful, and that given time and experience, will be looked back upon as "not as bad as I thought it was going to be."

Conclusion   For organizational change to take place effectively, I must first have an idea, an insight into why what we're doing now isn't working, and I must be able to articulate this clearly to my staff; a vision of what the change will be and the benefits of that change; then the dedication and strength of will to overcome the chaos; and, finally, the resources to provide those affected by the change with the knowledge, ability, and skills to prepare for their new functions, or roles. And, I must adhere to the old philosophy: *Form follows function.* I cannot change the structure of the organization (the organizational chart) without first changing the process. (An exception is when the numbers of "customers" declines; that is, the only change is a reduction in volume, not process.)

Change *can* be accomplished through sheer force; it will simply be very costly in terms of the time and effort needed to effect the change, and in staff turnover. The sad part is that with forced change, the staff I'm going to lose will be the high achievers, those producing at the 80 to 90 percent level. The ones who are working just to get a paycheck, at a 20 to 30 percent level of productivity, will stay—they're very good at knowing just exactly how much they have to do to keep their jobs, and no more.

C A S E   S T U D Y

A SUCCESSFUL CHANGE

*Judith M. Jenkins, M.S.N., R.N., a clinical nurse specialist affiliated with a large, urban, tertiary-care hospital, had an idea, a vision, of how a change in the process of patient care could increase quality of care, would not affect the outcome, and would decrease the cost of care. A pretty unbeatable combination.

BACKGROUND

Protocol in this large, urban hospital required that all patients who underwent carotid endarterectomies spend 24 hours in intensive care following post anesthesia surgical recovery (PASR). Patients who had an uneventful PASR experience consistently did not de-

A SUCCESSFUL CHANGE Concluded

velop complications in intensive care. Having made this observation, Ms. Jenkins reviewed the literature and five years of hospital records to support her observation with objective data.

From this observation came an idea, a vision. Why couldn't patients who did not develop complications in PASR bypass intensive care and be admitted directly to the postop vascular surgery unit? She organized her proposal around the three components of interest to her varied audiences (hospital administrators, vascular surgeons, nursing, and ancillaries): cost, quality of care, and outcome.

PROPOSAL

Admit patients with an uneventful PASR experience directly to the postop vascular surgery unit, by protocol and upon assessment and recommendation by a resident physician.

Quality of care will be enhanced as evidenced by a decrease in the stress experienced by patients and family members who must undergo a stay in intensive care; and an increase in the time devoted to patient and family teaching available on the postop unit. *Outcome* will not be affected. And, *costs* will be reduced by $xx due to elimination of a day in intensive care and the shortened hospital length of stay multiplied by the number of days saved per year.

Hospital administration supported the proposal *provided* the surgeons agreed to change the protocol.

Vascular surgeons, who had the authority to change the protocol for these patients, were interested, *but* with a caveat: There must be a pilot period followed by a thorough evaluation; *and* participation in the protocol had to be voluntary for the pilot period, following a postop assessment of the patients by a resident physician.

Nurse managers were reluctant, but agreed to support the pilot *if* they could add more RNs to their staff, provide training for the care of patients with that level of acuity, and provide additional support for the evening, night, and weekend shifts. (Where do we assign nurses with the least experience? Evenings and nights.)

Administration agreed to the increase in staff and training even though it was to be a pilot program with voluntary participation. Upon completion and evaluation of the pilot program, administration, vascular surgeons, nursing management, and nursing staff recommended a permanent change in the protocol, and that the protocol would now be automatic, upon patient assessment by a resident physician.

When I interviewed *Judy Jenkins, who initiated this change, and asked her, "To what do you attribute your success?", she said, "It was a team effort; I didn't do it all by myself." Then I asked, "How did you go about getting the team to work together as a team rather than as a collection of individuals?" She replied:

> I think you have to build confidence, build on their strengths, and also see to it that each person gets something out of it. What was of most interest to administrators, surgeons, and nurses was what we focused on. For instance, administration, while truly caring about patient satisfaction, was interested in the reduction in length of stay and dollars spent.

Analysis of a Successful Change

*Judy Jenkins was successful because she applied several principles that have stood the tests of time and experience.

1. *Interaction with others is more effective when we meet them where they are rather than where we want them to be.*
2. *Any effort to implement change will be met by a degree of resistance proportional to the meaning of the change to the person.*
3. *Communication is most effective when the speaker and the audience speak the same language.*

C A S E   S T U D Y

A DISASTROUS CHANGE

A large, urban teaching hospital purchased a program designed to convert the hospital from the apothecary method of drug administration to unit dose. The hospital also purchased a computer system, the first program of which was compatible with unit dose. In addition to the physician's being able to enter medication orders for direct transmission to the pharmacy, the computer would automatically print out a new MAR at midnight, every night. And, two unit dose carts would be placed on every nursing unit.

The nurse charged with the training for and implementation of these two programs developed the classes, subjected the classes to

A DISASTROUS CHANGE Concluded

peer review, and requested that the training be mandatory, to im-press upon the nursing staff the importance of attending.

Classes were scheduled around the clock to accommodate all three shifts. Despite the existence of a definite time when the com-puters would be activated and unit dose would go into effect, *and* the mandatory requirement to attend classes, attendance was sparse to nonexistent. Only about 30 percent of the staff had been trained and were ready when the two systems were activated. It was a true disaster.

Analysis of a Disaster

What happened? The nurse charged with training and implemen-tation violated several principles:

1. *Interaction with others is more effective when we meet them where they are rather than where we want them to be.* The nurse expert viewed the computers with their attendant programs as a toy, as well as relief from having to go behind medical stu-dents and interns to check their orders for accuracy (pharmacists would now do that). She also viewed unit dose as a giant leap for-ward in efficiency for the nursing staff. The presence of two carts on every nursing unit rather than the one centralized medicine room would put the meds closer to the patient rooms. And, to have the meds premeasured and prepackaged would save so much time now spent pouring meds.

The staff nurses and nurse managers viewed the new com-puter system with its attendant programs as more work. They also feared loss of control and an inability to monitor medical students and intern medication orders—a function that they had internal-ized as a right and responsibility. Unit dose was viewed as a throwback to functional nursing, with a medicine nurse (this hos-pital was in the throes of implementing primary nursing). The convenience of the medicine carts was lost on them.

2. *Any effort to implement change will be met by a degree of resistance proportional to the meaning of the change to the person.* The resistance to this perceived attack on their professional roles was evident through refusal to attend the training sessions.

3. *Communication is most effective when the speaker and the audience speak the same language.* The nurse expert was speaking the language of new and exciting; the nursing staff was speaking the language of denial and loss.

Conclusion   The nurse expert failed to ascertain how the target audience, nursing staff and managers, viewed these pending changes as a starting place for dialogue. Instead, she used an authoritarian approach as expressed in the request for mandatory attendance. The cost to the organization in time and effort to bring everyone up to speed on these two programs was enormous—and unnecessary had the nurse expert applied principles rather than relying on authority.

Who was this dumb? I was, Katie Mott. I did that all by myself—I cannot in good conscience blame another soul for this disaster. It was a "Significant Learning Experience."

If I were asked today to take on a similar task, I would agree to do it *with the provision* that I be allowed 30 days to do nothing but spend time with the nursing staff and managers to elicit their views of what these impending changes meant to them in order to start where they are and to be able to sell them on the benefits of the new programs—(What's In It for Me?).

We have taken apart change and put it back together again. And, we have seen how important it is to adhere to our basic principles. The principles will not let us down—we can only let ourselves down by ignoring them.

Time to move on and take apart and put back together again that abstract concept known as "communication."

The Art and Science of Language Skills

The Mandatory Chapter on Communications

I'm going to start this chapter with the communication wheel, or circle—whichever you call it—because I want you to know that I know it. So do you.

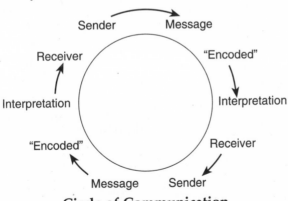

Circle of Communication

This is so-o-o-o repetitious. Been there. Done that. We know about the importance of the sender, encoding, the interpretation, and all that stuff. This model worked beautifully in the command-

and-control structure of yesteryear. It is inadequate to meet the leadership challenges facing us as we head toward the 21st century. We need something more. Therefore, we're again going to add depth to what we already know about communication—just as we did with motivation.

First, we're going to incorporate a model of communication that is far more useful to us as we seek to not only *empower* our staff to make their own decisions but expect them to actually *use* that power. *They must make their own decisions.* There is a difference between having power and using power, a profound difference.

Then, we're going to look at upward communications and ways to improve our ability to communicate with those to whom we report.

THE PARENT-ADULT-CHILD MODEL OF COMMUNICATION

We're going to add the parent-adult-child model of communication to what we already know.

Eric Berne is the father of the parent-adult-child school of communication. Berne wrote a book entitled *Games People Play* (New York: Grove Press,1964) in which he laid out for us a concept he called transactional analysis. His book was on the *New York Times* best-seller list for weeks and weeks and weeks—evidence of the degree of interest in what he had to say. (Slight digression: I went up into my attic and found that I have a first edition of this book! Are you suitably impressed? I'd be willing to bet that my first edition is worth at least 25 cents at any yard sale). He actually presented a very deeply thought-out psychoanalytic theory that is far beyond our interest. What *is* of interest to us is his view of the way we communicate with each other. He literally analyzed our transactions with each other—hence the name, *transactional analysis.* Clever, huh?

Berne was a disciple of Freud, and we'll recognize that in his work. He said that each of us has within us three people: a parent, an adult, and a child. (My husband would say, "At least." He says he never knows who's going to greet him when he comes home in the evening.)

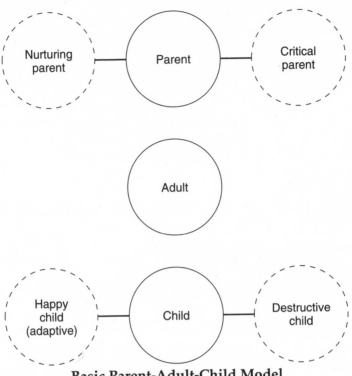

Basic Parent-Adult-Child Model

Each one us has within us a *parent*. In fact, we have two parents, a *nurturing parent* and a *critical parent*. The nurturing parent says, "You look tired. Why don't you take a few days off," or, "Don't worry about it; I'll take care of it." The critical parent says, "You got yourself into it—you should never have made that decision," or, "I'm just telling you this for your own good."

Some people call the critical parent the Sunday school of the mind because it is filled with shoulds and oughts.

Each one of us has within us an *adult*. The adult focuses on issues and problem solving. It isn't that there is no feeling or emotion in the adult, it's that the feeling and emotion are secondary to the issue. I think of Jack Webb and the old television show *Dragnet*. "Just the facts, ma'am." I also think of Mr. Spock and Data on *Star Trek*. "The issue is that we are not receiving our computer supplies in a timely manner, and when we don't get the supplies it affects our ability to plan a timely discharge for the patient. What can we do that will help to resolve this problem?"

And, each one of us has within us a *child*, for which we are grateful. Like the parent, the child also has two faces: a *happy child* and a *destructive child*. The happy child is the one who has fun at picnics, is able to "let her hair down," and enjoys the company of others. It is the happy child within us that has fun skiing down a mountain, or playing in the surf, or in my case finding new and old treasures at the flea market. The destructive child can be either openly rebellious, terribly dependent, or excessively compliant.

Thus, we can recognize Freud's superego, ego, and id.

Why Is the Parent-Adult-Child Model of Communication Important?

Let's look again at our situational leadership model and see how we use these communication styles.

Adult *Delegate*	Relationship
Adult/Parent *Participate*	Relationship/Task
Parent/Adult *Sell*	Task/Relationship
Parent *Tell*	Task

Parent-Adult-Child Model and Situational Leadership

Tell

Isn't this a very parental role—telling people what to do? I'm also not too interested in the *relationship* that you and I have at this level. What I am interested in is that we have a clear understanding of what *tasks* need to be accomplished. (The last time I was involved in a code I don't remember anyone asking me how I felt about it. We had a task to do and someone was barking orders.)

Sell

I'm still in a parent role—teaching you and coaching you. However, I acknowledge that there is another adult present. I do that anytime I say "because." When I'm trying to "sell" you on an idea, or another way of doing something, I am acknowledging that you may or may not agree with me. In other words, we have shared power, even though at this level I still have a bit more power than you. I'm still making the decisions, though you now have the ability to influence my decisions by presenting me with objective data.

We still have some tasks to master; however, we are beginning to develop and build a relationship. After all, I care enough to say *why* something is important and deserving of our attention.

Participate

I'm beginning to turn the power over to you. You are making the decisions, even though as the parent I have not abandoned you. I am still there to support you. The adult is dominant; the parent is supportive. The relationship assumes a higher degree of importance even though we have a few tasks to clean up. (Recall, this is where we are out there putting into practice the knowledge, ability, and skills we learned in *sell*.)

Delegate

And, now we've gotten there—the power is all yours. This is a purely adult form of communication that focuses on the relationship. I am not needed as parent, and the tasks have been mastered. You are making the decisions, within boundaries; and you are accountable for those decisions.

Communication from my parent says that I am exerting power over another person. Let's look again at our situational

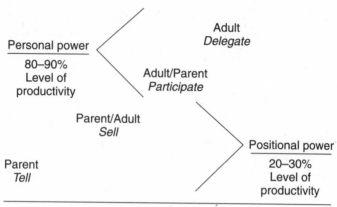

Parent-Adult-Child Model and Power

leadership model and see how this communication style correlates with power.

When I manage within the tell or sell levels, my parent is dominant and I am using *positional power.* (Recall that I can expect a level of productivity of 20 to 30 percent when I manage from these positions.)

When I manage within the participate or delegate levels, my adult is dominant and I am using *personal power.* (Recall that I can expect a level of productivity of 80 to 90 percent when I manage from these positions.)

What does this model of communication tell us that we didn't already know?

Everything!

Berne's essential message, and lesson for us, is that if I communicate with you as a parent to a child, you will respond to me as a child to a parent. It is such a profound message in its simplicity. If I want you to make independent, or interdependent, decisions as an adult, I must communicate with you adult to adult.

Why? Not because it is right or wrong. *I'm going to do it because It is more effective.*

We illustrated in Chapter 1, with our case study of Ms. Gregory and Dr. Jackass, how much more effective it was to support Ms. Gregory as an adult than to be a nurturing parent and treat her like a child.

Kinds of Transactions

Berne describes three kinds of transactions: complementary, crossed, and ulterior.

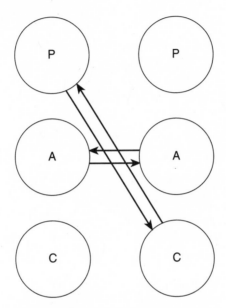

Complementary Transactions

Complementary Transaction

Complementary ego states are talking to each other. Sample complementary transactions include:

1. "I want this office cleaned up *now!*" "Yes, *ma'am!*" (Critical parent to child, compliant child to critical parent.) We *are* communicating. We are using positional power to get the other person to do what needs to be done.

2. "This office wouldn't pass muster with the fire department. What can we do about it?" "I have some time; I'll do the filing." (Adult to adult, adult to adult.) We *are* communicating. We are using personal power to get the other person to do what needs to be done.

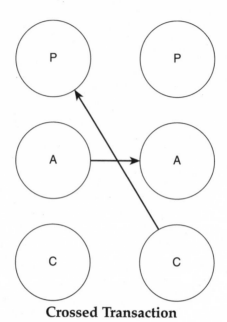

Crossed Transaction

Crossed Transaction

We end up with *no communication* because we have two separate and distinct messages. A sample crossed transactions includes:

1. "We've been asked to increase our home visits from a mean of 4.2 per day per nurse to 6 per day, in keeping with national standards." "Great! Doesn't anyone care about the quality of care around here? Am I the only one?" (Adult to adult, rebellious child to parent.)

Note: There is no communication. These are two separate issues: the number of home visits per day and quality of care.

Ulterior Transaction

There is *no communication* because there are two separate and distinct messages, and one of them is hidden. Sample ulterior transactions include:

1. "I just *looove* managed care." (Said with hands on hips and a scowl on her face.) The real message is that

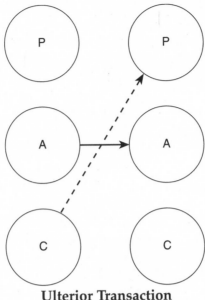

Ulterior Transaction

delivered with body language—and that message says she *hates* managed care.

2. "Critical paths may be a great idea, but they mean I have to learn to chart by exception—another thing to learn." Anytime we hear the *but* word we can discount anything that is said before the *but*. The true message here is the hidden one; what really counts is that she is going to have to learn one more thing.

> **Remember that everyone you meet wears an invisible sign. It reads, "Notice me. Make me feel important."**
>
> **H. Jackson Brown, Jr.**

Most adults maintain a balance between interacting from the parent, adult, or child part of the self. When I'm being a parent I am certainly a different person than when I am being childlike, or even child*ish*. There is almost a stimulus-response type of interaction that occurs when I address you as a parent to a child—you *respond* as a child. It is so predictable it's almost like magic! Likewise, when a child petitions my parent for help, I am almost programmed to provide that help—to rush in to fix that problem, whatever it is.

The adult ego state is sometimes referred to as the "executive position" because this is the seat of my rational, problem-solving self. While I want to spend most of my time here, I don't want to shut out my child or parent. If I stayed in my adult all the time I would never react emotionally to any issue, would probably be a workaholic, always be rational, and would be extremely dull and boring. I've been called a lot of things—*never* dull and boring!

This concept is important to us as we attempt to move staff into decision-making roles; that is, *staff* are going to make decisions as adults. I am *not* going to continue to make the decisions as a parent. Nor am I going to continue to respond as the parent to the child who is asking me to solve the problem. As long as I am willing to solve all the problems, my staff is more than likely willing to stand aside while I solve them.

————

Let's look at another transaction, and you plot it out on the diagram below.

Sample Transaction
"Our staff meetings have begun to drift along without a seeming purpose and are taking an inordinate amount of time. Beginning next week, we'll have a structured agenda so that we'll all understand the stated purpose for the meeting." "Does that mean that I can't talk about anything unless I get your permission ahead of time? What if you don't want me to talk about it?"

Analysis Who is sending the message? Who is responding to the message? What kind of transaction is it? Complementary? Crossed? Ulterior?

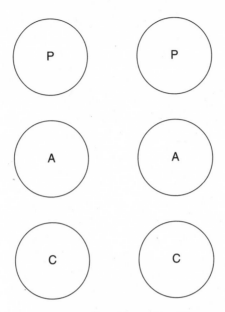

Transaction Exercise #1

Who is sending this message? (Adult)
To whom? (Adult)
Who is responding? (Child)
To whom? (Parent)

When we draw the arrows we have a *crossed transaction.*

Want another one?

Sample Transaction

"Why am I always the one who has to call Dr. Scott with news he doesn't want to hear?" "Because you do it so well. Go call him."

Analysis   Who is sending the message? Who is responding to the message? What kind of transaction is it? Complementary? Crossed? Ulterior?

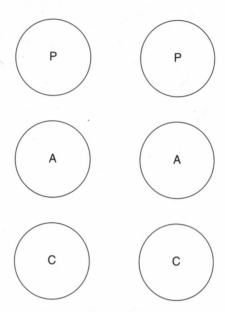

Transaction Exercise #2

Who is sending this message? (Child)
To whom? (Parent)
Who is responding? (Parent)
To whom? (Child)

When we draw the arrows we have a *complimentary transaction.*

This can be fun. Here are some blank circles for you to diagram a recent interaction of interest, especially one in which you were confused about the outcome.

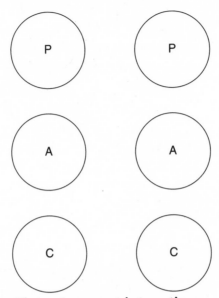

Plot out a recent interaction.

We're going to move on now to the second part of communication, which is, Who's Listening?

LISTENING

Probably the most important concept in communicating with others is *listening*. According to a team of professors at Loyola University in Chicago, listening is the most important skill a manager can possess (Alessandra, T., and Hunsaker, P. *Communicating at Work*. New York: A Fireside Book, 1993). And yet, we receive so little training to become good listeners.

I remember studying active listening when I was taking Psych Nursing. I thought that was something that applied to people with psychiatric, or as we would say today, mental health problems. I didn't know it was for all kinds of problems and was a skill that would be useful in management. I learned to transfer this skill from psychiatry to everyday life the hard way—the way most of us learn: Significant Learning Experiences. I also discovered that I wasn't *really* listening. Sometimes I was just waiting for the other person to stop talking so I could say what I wanted to say.

Why All This Emphasis on Listening?

- Managers spend 45 percent of their time (in communicating with others) in listening.

- We tend to use only 25 percent of our listening skills when we're listening to a talk that lasts for 10 minutes.

- We speak at a speed of 135 to 175 words per minute. We *listen* at 400 to 500 words per minute. Alessandra says we spend the difference in speaking time and listening time in "jumping to conclusions, daydreaming, planning a reply, or mentally arguing with the speaker" (p. 55).

- Active listeners exhibit an increase in blood pressure, pulse rate, and respiration.

- Our average effectiveness as listeners is 25 percent. This means that 75 percent of what we should be hearing, we're either not hearing or will be inclined to distort or forget later.

In his excellent book, *The 7 Habits of Highly Effective People* (New York: Simon and Schuster, 1993) Stephen Covey illustrates the *levels* of listening, with each higher level requiring more effort than the one before.

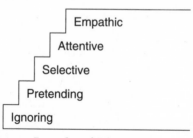

Levels of Listening

My goal is to be *attentive* or *empathic*, as the need arises. And I can see that these higher levels of listening require more than just a casual nod of the head and cursory attention. I'm going to have to work at it—exert that extra effort. As hard as I try, there are factors that work against me that I must try to overcome as I try to listen. Voncile M. Smith and Thelma A. Bass (*Communication for Health Professionals*. Philadelphia: J. B. Lippincott, 1979) have provided us with a clear and concise guide to these factors, and to our ability to select that which we want to hear.

Factors Affecting My Ability to Listen

- *Age:* The young and the old see the world through different lenses. Today's older worker may well have been a depression baby, or reared by parents who grew up in the depression, concerned with job security and fearful of change. Today's younger worker may thrive on the constant challenge of new technologies, be bored with the status quo, and prepared to change careers five times in her lifetime. Each one will hear differently a statement like, "We'll be attending classes for cross training in preparation for our reengineered workplace."
- *Sex:* I really do believe that men and women are from different planets, at least most of us are. My husband hates to go out for lunch—he'd rather stay in his office and eat leftovers. The women in his office love to go out for lunch. Occasionally my husband doesn't have leftovers to eat. When that happens the women consistently ask if he'd like to join them in going out for lunch. Just as consistently he declines the invitation and says, "Bring me something." The interaction then goes something like this: "What do you want?" "Where are you going?" "What do you want?" "Where are you going?" He has solved this dilemma: He has constructed a chart that requests that, if the women go to Pizza Hut he would like . . . If the women go to McDonald's he would like . . . , and so on. This chart is now on the bulletin board in the kitchen area. The women want to be nurturing and to take care of him and he doesn't want to be a bother to them—they aren't speaking the same language.
- *Education:* While the content of my message may be the same, I will alter its presentation partly dependent on the

educational level of the audience. While I might say, "q.i.d." to another nurse or health care worker, I would probably say, "four times a day" to a layperson.

- *Physiological Conditions:* This phrase makes us think about problems with seeing and hearing. There can also be problems with attempting to hold the attention of someone who has a headache, is nauseated, or is sleepy due to working all day and being up all night with a sick child.

- *Social and Economic Background:* The person with inherited wealth hears "expensive medication" differently from the person who lives payday to payday. It is my job to say, "By expensive, I mean . . ."

- *Status:* In a perfect world status wouldn't matter. In the real world it frequently does matter. My responsibility is to ensure that I honor status when it is important. The governor of the state is going to hear the same message about health care differently than the newly arrived immigrant. Likewise, I will attach a different meaning to a message from the governor about health care than I will the newly arrived immigrant because of my perception of their differing understanding of the issues. Not more or less meaning—just different.

Selective Actions by Listeners

Listeners are wonderful. Just because someone is looking at me with what appears to be an intent expression on her face doesn't mean she is hearing what I'm saying. We are all guilty of listening selectively. We listen; we don't hear.

Selective Exposure

A synonym might be "convenient deafness." We are simply inclined to hear those things we want to hear and to discount, or not to hear, those things we don't want to hear. We can all probably cite the example of a person with self-described hearing loss who professes to profound deafness—until we mention his name. Then his ears perk up and he hears every word we say about him. Let's take the statement, "The purpose of case management is to ensure an orderly movement through the system for the benefit of the patient." The person from the finance office will hear "cost-effective"; the case manager will hear "coordinated care"; and the patient will hear "I'm not going to get lost in the system."

Selective Attention

We can only "attend to" so many stimuli at one time. When we are inundated with many stimuli we selectively choose those to which to pay attention. I find that I can keep the television set on a news channel all day to provide background noise while I'm working in my home, and that does not distract me—it is, instead, a comforting sound. I cannot keep the radio on a music station, or play CDs, because I would be distracted—I would want to listen to the music. This is the most important reason for having staff conferences in a quiet office: to decrease the number of stimuli competing for attention. It is also a good reason to defer heavy educational programs until after the Christmas/Hanukkah/Kwanza season—our target audience will be focused on preparation for the festivities of the season, not new learning.

Selective Perception

We attach meanings to words, phrases, or messages that have their origin in our knowledge, beliefs, values, and experiences. The experienced worker who has been through many changes will attach a different meaning to "reengineer" than the newer, younger worker who has not had this experience. If I am conditioned by my union to view administration as the "enemy," then I am going to perceive their every move with suspicion. If I am conditioned by administration to believe that the only purpose for unions is to make work and to protect outmoded jobs, then I am going to be suspicious of any questions the shop steward has about the proposed changes.

Selective Retention

I tend to retain those bits of information I want to remember. I will especially retain messages about myself that reinforce my self-image and reject those that detract from it.

When I incorporate these factors into our parent-adult-child model of communication, I become a better listener and much better at ascertaining where my listener is (so that I can start where she is rather than where I want her to be). Keeping these attributes at a conscious level helps me to avoid a very costly mistake—making assumptions.

*June Bowman, M.S.N., R.N., believes strongly that one of the most important skills we *must* have, as managers, is the ability to listen. She said:

> I think there is a lot of symbolism in communication that we tend to forget about, and my biggest advice to managers (and advice I need to take myself, sometimes) is to wipe everything else that is on my agenda out of my mind and to try to give that person my undivided attention. If I don't do that, then they start telling me things and my mind is wandering off on something else, and I don't always hear what it is that they are *really* [italics mine] saying. Sometimes I have to read between the lines: What is it they are trying to tell me? If I don't put forth the effort to have that kind of communication, then they get up to leave and I've missed the whole point.
>
> In watching really good leaders I think that is a specific thing that always sticks out about them. They give you their undivided attention—as if you're the only person in the world when they're interacting with you. That always makes you feel really good. Hey, this person really does care about what I'm saying. I think the communication is much more open when the other person is getting that kind of attention.

Skills to Help with Active Listening

When I am listening to another person my goal is to respond to what is *actually* being said. This will involve the effort we discussed earlier. I must focus my attention entirely on the other person. I must concentrate on what the person is *saying* (the words) and what the person is *doing* (tone of voice, loudness or softness of voice, facial expression, body language, etc.). The purpose of this effort is to assess for a "fit" between what the person is saying and what the person is doing. Actions speak louder than words.

My goal is to engage the other person in conversation *without making her defensive.* I want us to communicate as adults—not parent and child.

Example Sue states, "I don't care what you say. They never keep their word." Her body language includes fidgeting with a pen, tapping her foot, and a strained expression on her face.

Goal To uncover the issue and deal with it as adults.
     Let's diagram that statement:

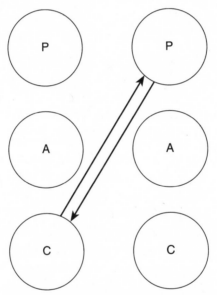

Selective Listening (Arguing)

That message is coming from the destructive child to the nurturing parent and is saying, "Fix it." I can't fix it. I want the interaction to be adult-adult. If I challenge Sue's belief system by arguing with her child, all I will accomplish will be to engage in a "Did too," "Did not" argument guaranteed to get us nowhere. I want to avoid making Sue defensive. I want to move this interaction to the adult. How do I do that?

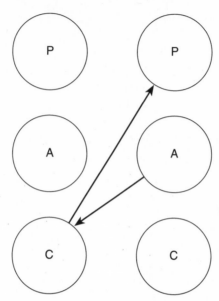

Using Active Listening to Get to an "Adult" Interaction

All I have to do is to *acknowledge Sue's child*. I don't have to agree with Sue; I don't have to approve of her statement; I just have to acknowledge that Sue's child is having problems. I can do that any one of a number of ways. Here are a few.

1. *Paraphrasing*
   "In other words . . ."
   "What I hear you saying is . . ."
   "Sounds like . . ."

2. *Clarifying*
   "Is it like this all the time or just some of the time?"
   "Could you be more specific?"
   "Could you say that another way?"

3. *Feedback*
   "If I understand you correctly, you're saying that . . ."
   "You're feeling . . ."

4. *Give permission*

"Most anyone would be angry if she thought she wasn't hearing the truth."

5. *Reflecting (another form of feedback)*

"It's rough to feel singled out."

"Security is really important."

"It's really important to be able to trust our employers."

Each one of these skills acknowledges the child in a nonjudgmental way and keeps the door open for a continuation of the conversation—an opportunity to move the interaction to the adult level.

There is a fundamental reason for acknowledging the child. We believe that we are more effective when we begin where the other person is. This is where Sue is at this moment—in her child. Now, and *only now,* when I acknowledge the child, is Sue ready to give up her child and join me in the adult role to identify and resolve the problem.

This is how we did it.

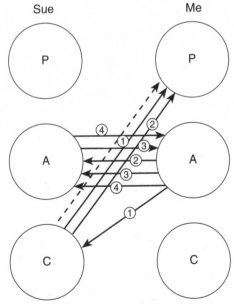

Analysis of My Interaction with Sue

1. *Sue:* I don't care what you say. They never keep their word.
1. *Me:* Ouch. Sounds like you think someone's not telling the truth. (Paraphrasing)
2. *Sue:* That's right—that's exactly what I think.
2. *Me:* Could you be more specific? What is one thing that you have heard that you don't believe to be true? (Clarifying)
3. *Sue:* Well, you said that we would all get new job descriptions, and they said there wouldn't be any pay cuts, but I don't believe 'em.
3. *Me:* So, you're afraid you're going to get a cut in your salary? (Feedback)
4. *Sue:* Yes.
4. *Me:* Let's look at what is actually written in the memo. (Adult-to-adult communication looking now at the problem rather than the feeling attached to the problem)

Analysis of Interaction

By beginning where Sue was, in her child, I was able to guide her to her adult ego state. Sue and I can now deal with the true issue, which is whether or not her pay will be cut rather than the perception that "someone out there" was lying to her.

Danger! Danger! Danger!

Active listening is a *skill to be used when it is needed!* We do not perform an appendectomy on a perfectly healthy adult. We do not use active listening casually.

In fact, I can guarantee that I won't have any friends left by the end of the week if I use active listening casually—if I attempt to uncover some hidden meaning where none exists. If I ask, "Where's the bathroom?" I don't want to hear, "It's really hard to have to go and not know where the bathroom is." I might be tempted to tell you where to put your active listening.

What I *do* want to do is to develop antennae. I want a sensitivity to my staff that will automatically trigger a reaction on my part to hidden messages or strong feelings I need to pursue further. The antennae will emerge on their own (and invisibly) as I listen attentively (the level of listening just below empathic).

Practice Session

Using the parent-adult-child circles, practice diagramming the following statements and your responses to them. Remember, our goal is to be empathic, to feel *with*, not *for*; to walk in the other person's shoes for a half second; to begin where the other person is. We definitely want to avoid making the other person defensive—guaranteed to happen if we challenge the belief by saying, "That's not true," or any other statement designed to contradict the belief. People who are defending the self against a perceived threat are doing just that—defending. They are not problem solving.

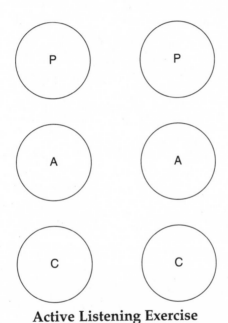

Active Listening Exercise

Sample Statements that Are Candidates for Active Listening

"Working hard doesn't count. The old-timers get all the breaks around here."

"You're always picking on me. Don't I ever do anything right?"

"What I think doesn't matter. They're going to do what they want to do anyway."

"That's a joke" (said in reference to a promise).

UPWARD COMMUNICATION

My observation and experience through the years have led me to the conclusion that the reason many of us have difficulty communicating with our administrators or line officers is that we aren't speaking the same language.

One of my biggest challenges is to secure resources for my staff. My colleague, *John C. McDonald, M.S., R.N., expressed this very succinctly. When I asked him to describe to me his most important function as a manager, he responded,

> I want my staff to know that they don't work for me; I work for them. My most important job is to remove the barriers which people or forces put in their way which prevent them from doing a good job.

To "remove the barriers," John must be able to truly listen to me, and I must be able to communicate my needs to him.

To communicate my needs to the person(s) to whom I report I must speak the same language. It's that simple. The same principle of management applies: If I want to be more effective I will meet the other person where he is rather than where I want him to be. It's just as applicable to my relationship with my administrator as it is to my relationship with my staff and peers.

I wouldn't dream of going to a foreign country and attempting to be understood by raising the level of my voice and speaking more slowly and distinctly. I would be called an "ugly American," and rightly so. Raising the level of my voice and speaking more slowly and distinctly won't help me with my administrator either; it would be rude and condescending. I must speak the language of administration—the language of business.

Some nurse, way back when (this one wasn't Flossie) decided to take the scientific decision-making process and put other words to it. They were *assess, plan, implement, and evaluate.* She called it the "nursing process." We now had our own language and declared ourselves to be very special. This separate language has not served us well. We must return to our roots and to the language of science (and by extension, business).

THE DECISION-MAKING PROCESS

I have taken the nursing process and placed it on one side of the page, and placed the comparable business language on the other side of the page. When I look at this I can see that I do understand business—I'm just not speaking the language. Given these compare-and-contrast columns, I am now prepared to be bilingual—to speak the language of nursing and of business—and in the same breath!

THE DECISION MAKING PROCESS

The Nursing Process	Scientific Decision-Making Process
Assess	Observation
Review of systems	Review of literature
Socioeconomic status	External environment
Psychologic status	Internal environment
Problem statement	Problem statement
Plan	Proposal
Purpose	Purpose
Goal	Proposed outcome
Action	Proposed action
Patient	Strengths
Staff	Weaknesses
Physician	Resources needed
Other	Cost/Benefit analysis
Time Frame	Relationship to mission Statement/strategic plan
Implement plan	Implementation plan
Evaluate effectiveness	Evaluate effectiveness

When my purpose is to seek resources from my administrator, I'm not going to say that I *assessed* the situation. I'm going to say that I *made an observation* that I supported in the literature.

I have conducted *reviews of the literature.* So have you. I won't ever forget, "The skin is the body's first line of defense." I got that by reviewing the literature. I'm going to read everything I can get my hands on. I'll start with the nursing literature; then I'll find the same problem in the medical literature (if it's a clinical problem); or, I'll find it in the management literature (if it's a management problem). I'm going to become an expert on that particular issue *before I ever define it as a problem.*

The *external environment* is simply a reflection of what is going on all over the country (or world, if it's applicable) with respect to the particular topic under study. It's helpful to be able to relate what's happening to agencies similar to the one with which I am affiliated. (What is being done in a large, urban university teaching hospital is not necessarily applicable to a home health agency in a rural area.)

Then I want to look at the *internal environment.* This is an objective look at the resources available internally, within my own agency, which can be drawn upon to address the problem. What are we already doing? What do we need to be doing? Can we do it? Do we have the physical resources (staff and supplies)? Do we have the financial resources (money for capital improvements, addition of staff)? Do we have the support of important constituency groups (physicians, nurses, community leaders)?

When I find a gap between what *should* be done, what *is* being done, and what *can* be done, I then have a *problem*—and only then.

Having sold my administration on the possibility of improving quality of care and outcomes, and of reducing costs, I am now ready to develop my proposal. It is exactly like a nursing care plan.

First, I must state the purpose—why do I want to do this? The *purpose* will take the form of an outcome—what I hope to achieve.

Then I'm going to suggest a method of *action* designed to achieve that *outcome.* More than one method of action is a plus (because it's very rare that there is only one way to get to Rome). This is where we deviate from the nursing care plan. We suggested one plan of care for the patient and supported that plan with principles. (As an instructor I can tell you that I was already staying up until 2:00 AM to read care plans. I didn't want to stay up all night to read about options—I just wanted to know that your thought processes were logical, orderly, and sequential.) Now I must cite the *strengths* and *weaknesses* of the plan. Number one, no plan is perfect. Number two, identifying the weaknesses up front provides us with the information we need to overcome the weaknesses, if indeed we can.

Next I must be very honest about the *resources* needed to implement this program. If I have done a thorough job of analyzing the internal environment, this part will be easy.

Then, I must do a *cost/benefit analysis.* Baccalaureate and graduate programs in nursing are now including managed care as part of the curriculum. Those of us who graduated before the days of managed care might not know how to do a cost/benefit analysis. Also gone are the days of being able the say that the benefit is "community goodwill." There is going to have to be a dollar figure attached.

If I don't know how to do a cost/benefit analysis, then I'm going to make an appointment to see the chief financial officer, pick up my calendar on the way out the door, and request that I be taught how to do this. It isn't difficult. If I am told that it is terribly complex and would take a long time, I'm going to open my calendar and say, "Good. When can we schedule the first half hour?"

I must, in my proposal, be able to relate what I want to do to the strategic plan and to the mission statement. If it doesn't relate to both of those I need to go back to the drawing board. It must relate to the strategic plan and to the mission statement.

The *implementation plan* is a piece of cake. This is simply the how-to. Who to hire, when to train, by whom and for what? Will there be a pilot program? I must be very detailed with this plan. I must provide a firm foundation.

And finally, I must have a plan for *evaluation* of the effectiveness of the program, with the stated outcome as the benchmark.

That's business-think, and it's very effective. It's very logical, sequential, and orderly. And all I've done is taken the nursing process, which applies to a bio-psycho-social being composed of a number of interacting systems, and applied it to the interrelated systems within an organization.

Getting the Attention of My Administrator When I Have a Problem

The first thing I must do when I want to communicate with my administrator about *anything* is find out what is of interest to my administrator. We're back to **Principle 2: Interaction with others is** more effective when we meet them where they are rather than where we want them to be.

Every administrator has an agenda—a particular area of interest. My job is to find out what that is. If it is the budget, that's the first thing I want to talk about when we meet. Because *nothing else that I have to say will be heard until I address the administrator's agenda.* He or she will be sitting there nodding politely (hopefully), but won't hear a word I say until I say, "Money." Recall selective listening.

Staff who are involved in direct patient care and report to me need to know that the first thing I want to hear about is the patients. I won't hear another word they say until they tell me about the patients. I have an obligation to let the staff in on that little secret when I establish the foundation—when I tell them who I am and what they can expect of me. I'm not going to assume that my administrator is going to remember to do that for me. I'm going to take it upon myself to say, "When I reported to the former administrator, the first thing he wanted to know about was my status with respect to my department's goals and objectives. What would you like to discuss first?" I cannot read minds and it's dangerous to assume.

M. A. Allison and E. Allison (*Managing Up, Managing Down.* New York: Simon and Schuster, 1984), using their experience as a guide, developed a *Reporting V.* It serves as a guide for what is most important to administrators.

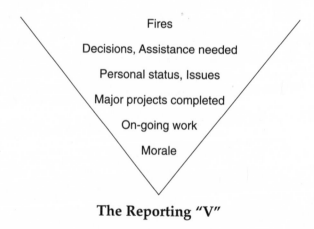

Fires

Decisions, Assistance needed

Personal status, Issues

Major projects completed

On-going work

Morale

The Reporting "V"

At the very top of the *V*, deserving attention first, is any emergency, represented by the word, *FIRES*. Where is staff morale? At the very bottom. Administration doesn't want to hear about staff morale. That's my problem. That's why they hired me.

What do I do when I think it is a problem. How can I be heard? Let's walk through this, applying what we have learned so far about communication.

Let's say that, under the pressures of managed care, my administrator is obsessed with costs. Remembering **Principle 2: Interaction with others is more effective when we meet them where they are rather than where we want them to be, and Principle 6: Communication is most effective when the speaker and the audience speak the same language,** and also understanding that nobody does anything for nothing, I'm going to discuss staff morale within the context of money. It isn't going to be difficult because if staff morale really *is* a problem there will be symptoms that led me to this conclusion. My approach to my administrator might go something like this:

I have made an observation.

Mr. Patrick, I've reviewed my budget figures for the past month and I see that I am way over for overtime and for temporary help.

Comparable to a literature review—I'm going to cite objective data to support my observation.

I have examined the variables that contribute to overtime and to temporary help and these are my findings. I've looked at the patient census, case mix, ALOS, and DRG mix by age, sex, and payor (Medicare, Medicaid, private insurance, etc.). I can find no significant difference between last month and all of FY 19—. I've also looked at the number of procedures the patients are requiring, the number of medications by route of administration and the number of needed interventions by ancillary departments. I can find no significant difference between last month and all of FY 19—. And, I've looked at staff mix, nurse-patient ratio, and even physician mix. And I can find no significant difference between last month and all of FY 19—.

There is, however, a significant different in the rate of absenteeism. It is much higher and the reasons given for being absent are so varied that it cannot be attributed to an epidemic or natural disaster of any kind.

I have identified the problem.

The conclusion I have reached is that the high rate of absenteeism and dependence on overtime and temporary help can be directly attributed to poor morale. This poor morale, in turn, is related to the staff's insecurity about the pending reorganization within our facility.

I have suggested a solution.

What I want to do is to address the underlying cause of the absenteeism, which is poor morale. In order to do this I must have information, information, information, etc.

I have stated the expected outcome and a method of evaluation.

Correcting the morale problem will result in a decrease in absenteeism, overtime, and temporary help, and that, in turn, will result in a net cost savings of $xx."

I do not guarantee that this approach will bring about the information I've requested. I *do* guarantee that it will increase my chances of getting it (Expectancy theory. The reward is a net decrease in cost, the effort is information, information, information, and the chances are better than 50 percent). Nobody does anything for nothing.

I have applied two of my basic principles, as well as knowledge gained from motivation theory.

There is an added bonus to this approach. The next time a project comes up that requires leadership, the administrator is likely to say, "Put Katie is charge. She knows the way I think." It's just like magic.

A final note: This is not manipulative and it is not gamey; it is just plain smart.

We've established a situational leadership framework within which we can be very direct about our expectations, teach or coach our staff in the needed knowledge, ability, and skills, and ensure that they have the support they need to function at their highest possible level. We've also added depth to what we know about motivation, applied motivational concepts to behavior modification, and have seen that the same principles that support our effectiveness in a stable environment also apply when we're in the midst of phenomenal change. And, we've now had a thorough look at communication: upwards, downwards, and sideways.

If we lived in a perfect world we could stop right here. We would have all the knowledge and skills that we need to be effective leaders and managers. Most of us, however, are blessed with staff who stand out and require our extra attention. Probably somewhere in the neighborhood of 20 percent of our staff create 80 percent of our problems; they also graciously endow us with 80 percent of our headaches. Who are they? The difficult people. The remainder of the book is dedicated to this infamous group.

Read on.

7

Difficult People

In Which We Discuss the 20% of People Who Cause 80% of Our Headaches

In a perfect world we would all be easygoing, fun to be around, eager to cooperate with each other and with authority figures and to live within the constraints imposed upon us by society. Fortunately, or unfortunately (somewhat dependent on how much variety we like in life), we don't live in a perfect world. Some people are just plain hard to get along with, and *very* difficult to manage.

The two personality types that seem to create the most problems for us are the *aggressive person* and the *great manipulator*.

Most people want to live up to our expectations, and nobody does anything for nothing. Remember that? If these principles are true, and I believe that they are, then there must be a reason for people to be difficult to get along with, that is, to be aggressive or manipulative. Especially since it is so much easier to cooperate and collaborate on a positive relationship—one in which everyone wins. Why, then, do some people do it the hard way, making life difficult for themselves as well as us?

In general, people who are aggressive, hostile, and intimidating are responding to their own anger. Therefore, if I understand the dynamics of anger, that should strengthen my ability to interact positively with aggressive people. Understanding the *why* of anger does *not* imply that it is OK to deal with it inappropriately—that is, in a manner that is disrespectful to another.

Others who are whiny, complainy, and manipulative are also aggressive. They just display their aggressiveness in their own unique way. Manipulators are more complex, however, and require that I superimpose the concept of trust on what I already know about anger. Again, understanding the *why* of manipulation does *not* mean that it's OK to manipulate—it just helps me deal with it more effectively.

So, we're going to proceed this way. First we'll look at anger and the continuum of responses to anger, including aggression, and how to deal effectively with each one of these responses. Then we'll look at the underlying, faulty belief system of the manipulator and what is effective and not effective with her (or him). Our goal throughout is to interact with the aggressor or manipulator from a position of caring and respect for her (or him)—*never* to demean or to put down the other person. Ready? Let's go.

ANGER

Anger is, essentially, the bodily response, the tension I feel when a goal that is designed to get one of my basic human needs met is denied. What differentiates anger from Selye's fight-or-flight response is the feeling of *resentment—it isn't fair.* I've certainly heard myself saying that on occasion.

We feel anger at both physiological and psychological levels. Physiologically, we exhibit an increase in blood pressure, pulse rate, and respiratory rate. When I am angry, my pupils dilate (one of the reasons for the green eyeshades worn by poker players), salivation may increase, and I may even be nauseated. I might even become constipated, or conversely, have diarrhea. These are the responses we expect with the fight-or-flight phenomenon, and are primarily responses to the surge of adrenaline. (One of my sisters and I just look at each other when we find ourselves in anxiety- or tension-producing situations with

> Anger is a short madness.
>
> —Horace

a look that says, "Which one of us is going to go to the bathroom first?")

The psychological part of me is responding to the threat to self, and that threat can be perceived as having been directed to me at any one of a variety of levels. Maslow helps us here. While Maslow's is a theory of human motivation, it also provides me with a way of identifying the specific human needs I must have met to live a balanced, healthy life. I acknowledge that I have a basic human right to have those needs met and that when that right is thwarted by some dastardly deed, *I react.*

Let's take a look at Maslow's human motivational needs with a different focus.

- *Physiological:* Basic, like clean air, safe water, and adequate nutrients. When these are denied to me by virtue of someone else's actions I get angry. Think of Love Canal. The denial doesn't even really *have* to be caused by another person; natural disasters can have the same effect. It is the perception that "it isn't fair."

- *Safety and security:* Again, a basic need. I must feel safe and secure in my environment, whether that environment is a cave designed to protect me from ice storms and bears or one within which I am safe from threats to my psychological integrity— the self. When all else is gone all I have left is my self and *I must defend it.*

- *Belonging:* We are herd animals—it's that simple. Hermits are considered to be an unnatural rarity; that's what makes them such good copy for writers. There is safety in numbers, and I want to be included in those numbers. As a human I am fortunate to have several herds to which I can belong: the family at home, the family at work, the family at school, the family at church or synagogue, and so on. Kids in gangs are screaming at us, trying to get us to hear that this need will be met—if not at home, school, church or synagogue, or club, then in a gang.

- *Self-esteem:* Self-explanatory. I must feel good about myself—that I am OK.

- *Achievement:* I have a strong need to believe that my actions make a difference, that given the opportunity I can do something with my life, and that my time here on earth was not in vain.

What happens when the goal to meet one or more of these needs is blocked?

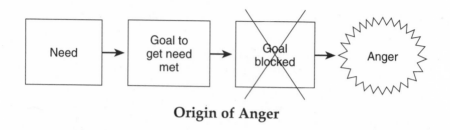

Origin of Anger

As a human I am a purposeful being—nobody does anything for nothing. I seek constantly to get my needs met. When I look at this diagram I can see that I have a *need* (which must be met), a *goal* (to get that need met), the goal is *blocked* (I can't get that need met for any one of a number of reasons), and I become *angry*.

Anger isn't good or bad; it just is. In fact, it can be beneficial. I may need that surge of adrenaline to prompt me to take action. It isn't the anger that is positive or negative, it is how I respond to it, what I do with the anger, how I handle it.

Gail W. Stuart and Sandra J. Sundeen (*Principles and Practice of Psychiatric Nursing*, 5th ed. St. Louis: C. V. Mosby, 1994) have suggested that we have a continuum of responses to anger, from constructive to destructive.

Continuum of Behaviors Used to Express Anger

Assertion

The assertive person has respect for self as well as others and is characterized by speaking in the "I." I, me, we, or us. The assertive person accepts accountability and responsibility for her own actions. The assertive person, while avoiding doing anything hurtful to another person, also speaks up to assert her right to live and work in an environment within which we respect each other. It is also a way to speak up now to avoid the inevitable increased tension that accompanies suppressed anger. If I ignore the anger it will not go away—I promise you, it won't. Assertiveness is the most constructive way of dealing with anger.

Frustration

Frustration is that uneasy feeling we have when something stands in the way of our accomplishing a goal. I will feel insecure and have a temporary feeling of angry disappointment. Even though I am frustrated, I am still problem solving, trying to find another way of getting my goal met—just not very effectively. The tension is beginning to be released. I might see that release of tension in myself or another person with agitation, pacing, difficulty sitting still, eating inappropriately, pressured speech—any one of a number of behaviors.

We all have a predictable pattern of behavior that tells those around us we're frustrated. I become bitchy and testy, and I am not ordinarily a bitchy or a testy person. The final straw is when the fingers on my left hand (not the right) spread apart and the fingers go through the hair, front to back. That's it. Katie's frustrated. And, I have let that be known loudly and clearly with body language.

I see Carol, who works for me, start sitting very still, becoming very quiet, and choosing her words carefully. That tells me that Carol, who is normally very vivacious and spontaneous in her interaction, is frustrated. Knowing that Carol is problem solving, but not very effectively, my appropriate role is to intervene to see if she wants or needs my help. The interaction might go something like this:

Me: Carol, the silence is deafening and I can see the withdrawal. That tells me there is a problem that is not resolving itself easily. I'm here and I'd like to help.
Carol: Thanks, Katie. I appreciate your interest. It's a personal problem and I'm dealing with it the best way I can. I'll be OK in two or three days.
Me: OK.

I will defend to the death Carol's right to deny me access to her brain uninvited. Neither I, nor anyone else, has that right. *Up to the point that Carol's frustration impacts adversely on patient care, or the performance of her job.* Then I have the right, responsibility, and authority to intrude despite her protests. Because now the issue is patient care or performance of her job, not her personal life. Patient care or her job performance can be adversely impacted in a variety of ways: Carol might be negligent or forgetful, or her behavior might be disruptive to the rest of the staff, causing an overall concentration on what's wrong with Carol rather than our purpose, whether that purpose is direct or indirect patient care.

Frustration is less constructive than assertiveness.

Passivity

While the assertive person has respect for self and others, the passive person has no respect for self. The passive person is characterized by an inability to express true feelings for fear of reprisal or rejection. I won't see her searching for other ways of reaching her goal. It isn't that the person isn't upset about some real or imagined threat to her integrity—she is just incapable of saying anything. The passive person is used to putting others' needs before her own. She might be heard to say, "I'm just glad I have a job," or, "I don't want to complain."

The passive person differs from the one who weighs the importance of any threat and casts aside those not worth fretting about. The passive person simple freezes and responds as if no threat had taken place. I may even be inclined to make the erroneous observation, "You're taking this well."

The passive person is entitled to display or not to display the feelings that surround her anger in the work situation. If she chooses not to, I hope that she has an alternate way of discharging the built-up tension to avoid a blowup later on. The passive person who does *not* deal with the hurt feelings, the anger, has the potential of becoming the *passive-aggressive* person who will then lash out at patients, co-workers, or at me.

One maladaptive coping mechanism used by many passive persons is *gunnysacking*. A gunnysack is a large burlap bag designed to hold produce, like potatoes. It works this way:

CASE STUDY

MYTH O'LOGIC HEALTHCARE CENTER: PASSIVE MARIA

Maria is a patient care assistant who has been employed on the same unit for 20 years. I have been her manager for six months. Maria works hard at being a team member and taking care of patients; she "minds her own business" and doesn't usually have much to say.

One day, walking down the hall, I see and hear Dr. Jackass screaming at Maria that she was rude to a patient. I know that

MYTH O'LOGIC HEALTHCARE CENTER: PASSIVE MARIA Concluded

Maria would never knowingly be rude to a patient. However, I also know Dr. Jackass's tendency to exaggerate, and I just shake my head and walk on.

During an informal, one-on-one meeting, I reveal to Maria that all patient care assistants will be required to undergo cross-training as we prepare for patient focused care. Maria quietly brings up her lack of formal education and expresses doubt in her ability to learn new skills and to be functional in a more flexible role. I disagree with that assessment of her abilities and reassure her that, of course she can.

In the course of a staff meeting, as I solicit feedback about the impact of the proposed changes, I have the following exchange with Maria:

Me: Maria, these changes are pretty profound for all of us. Most everyone else has had something to say about them. I'm interested in what you think about this.

Maria: Why do you care now? You never cared about how I felt before. Dr. Jackass screamed at me in the hall and said I'd been rude to his patient. I've never been rude to a patient in my life. You saw him and heard him say that and you didn't say a word.

You told me that I was going to have to be cross-trained so that I could do things other than vital signs, and answering lights, and doing I and O's. I told you I didn't have much education and I didn't know, after 20 years, whether I could learn something new, and you said, "Oh, of course you can."

And, another damn thing. Last August 10th at 2:00 PM you told me . . .

Analysis: Maria has gunnysacked. She kept piling the hurts into the gunnysack until the gunnysack exploded. Gunnysacks come equipped with fertilizer, warmth, and moisture. Anything we put in them is guaranteed to grow.

Does that mean that I have to pounce on everything that passive Maria says? No. It is pure application of my active listening skills. I must develop antennae that are sensitive to my staff (not *hyper*sensitive, not *in*sensitive—*sensitive*). Only then will I know when I need to follow up with Maria to take care of a problem now. Only then will I prevent the gunnysacking.

Chances are, if our lives are similar, and I think they are, Maria will say or experience something just as I am all but running down the hall, late to get to some event. I carry a little spiral notebook in my pocket for just such events. I'll write in it, "Maria and Dr. Jackass." Then, the first opportunity I have I'll get back with Maria and say, "Maria, that was a terrible thing Dr. Jackass said to you. I've never known you to be rude to anyone, much less a patient. Most anyone would be deeply hurt to hear that. How did you feel?" I give Maria permission to have feelings and to express those feelings.

Passivity is not a constructive way to respond to anger. In fact, it is self-destructive.

Aggression

At the next, less effective level of dealing with anger is aggression. It's interesting because aggressive people tend to think that they are very effective. In fact, very few persons want to work for them or with them.

I acknowledge the several theories that seek to explain aggression, ranging from Freud's primitive instinctual drive to the behaviorists' learned response. The one that seems to me to be rooted in common sense (as well as the scientific method) and is most helpful to me comes from the field of social psychology, or more accurately, social learning.

The aggressive person could probably best be described as a "bully." Intimidation is the name of the game, and others' rights and feelings are of little or no concern. "Steam roller" is another apt descriptor.

The aggressive person has no respect for the rights of others. Life is often perceived to be a battle within which we all fight to get our needs met. She expects to fight; she expects me to fight; and she has no respect for me when I don't. In fact, when I don't stand up for myself and challenge her, I confirm in her mind that she has no reason to respect me. In order for her to win, I must lose.

This is a difficult concept for us to buy as professional, caring people. I acknowledge that difficulty and live with it daily.

Aggressive behavior is frequently a coverup for a lack of self-confidence. I think of the old maxim "The best defense is a good offense." What is intended as a coping mechanism designed for self-protection and to hide her insecurities actually works against her by driving people away.

The aggressive person can be identified by certain common behaviors, which might include: a loud voice; a tendency to deliberately invade the other person's personal space (personal space equals arm's length) because it is intimidating; maintenance of eye contact until it becomes intrusive; threatening gestures; and, supererect posture designed to imply power and dominance.

> **Peace cannot be kept by force. It can only be achieved by understanding.**
>
> **—Albert Einstein**

The person who responds to anger with aggression is *not* problem solving. She's lashing out. That person is defending herself against what she perceives to be an attack on self—and this attack is manifested by a blocked goal. Denial of her needs is interpreted as an attack on self. The aggressive person is terribly narcissistic and self-centered. Her needs are the only ones that count; mine are not important.

I will hear a lot of, "she, he, them, they, and it." I will *not* hear "I," as in "I" am responsible. The aggressive person is inclined to blame all her troubles on some thing or person "out there." When I stop to think about it, it must be an awful feeling to believe that others are so in control of my life.

The most effective way of dealing with an aggressive person is to confront her, gently and firmly. Our nursing leaders, *June Bowman, *Frances Edwards, *Jean Johnson, *Mary Lou Jones, *John McDonald, and Judy Prater all agree that the aggressor must be confronted, though not in a destructive manner.

As an assertive person who is confronting the aggressive person, I will not lose sight of the respect I have for the other person. Only with consistent confrontation will the aggressive person gain respect for me and stop being aggressive—at least toward me and any others who consistently confront. This person may learn that she doesn't have to be defensive with me, because I respect her and will not take any action designed to hurt her, to threaten her concept of self. I *will* discuss her behavior—*not her.*

Aggression is a destructive way of dealing with anger.

Rage

The person who is in a true state of rage is out of control and *knows* it. It is a god-awful, gut-wrenching, miserable feeling. I think of a movie or TV show when some lunk is being thrown through a plate-glass window, and the window shatters (in slow motion) into three trillion little pieces. That's similar to the way the person in a true state of cold, blind rage feels—like his or her skin is going to shatter and he'll "fall apart in a trillion pieces." Please note that I said *cold, blind rage.*

If I don't work in an emergency department or psych unit I'll probably never see this. Staffs in these two areas are provided with specialized training in the management of persons who are out of control. That specialized training is far beyond the scope of this book and I don't want us to even *think* that we're experts in the management of rage just because we recognize it.

What I want to concentrate on is *safety*—for my staff and for our patients.

1. I want to have available a protocol that allows me to push a button to get help. I need several men to approach my out-of-control person slowly and directly in a show of force, or support. Their collective body language will say to the person, "You're OK. We're not going to let you fly into a trillion pieces—we're going to protect you." This is not a mean thing to do. It is a *kind* action. We are providing the external control to compensate for the enraged person's lack of internal controls.

Even small agencies, which do not ordinarily need or provide security forces, can have contingency plans. One small agency has a procedure wherein, upon signal, every man in the facility comes to the identified location. All we're talking about is a show of force, or support, or, as some would say, comfort.

2. I want to distract the person until the help arrives. By distracting the person I allow my staff to protect the patients and get help. If the person is moving, I want to move—backwards, in some sort of circular pattern to avoid backing myself into a corner. If the person is standing still I want to be still. I might lean against a piece of furniture in somewhat of a seated position—to lower my threat by assuming a less powerful position. I'll keep my legs positioned in the "lunge" position (one foot in front, back leg bent at the knee). I'll maintain eye contact and keep a well-modulated voice. This is one time that I want to "fake it 'til I make it." If I appear to be nervous and out of control, that will only heighten the fears my enraged person has.

I very seldom say, "Don't ever . . ." In this case I am saying, "Don't *ever* say to the person who is *truly* out of control. 'Get control of yourself!' " If she could, she would.

Caveat: If the out-of-control person has a gun or knife, take cover. Protect yourself the best way you can until help gets there.

I frequently hear that nurses see this behavior all the time in the operating room by temperamental surgeons. I would like to offer that they are *not* out of control, even though they *are* being aggressive. They know exactly what they are doing; they are having little-boy temper tantrums and they will continue to do it until they get the message that this is not acceptable behavior.

The same external controls we use with our person in a true state of rage can, and have been, used effectively with petulant surgeons. Upon a signal, every available nurse, scrubbed and unscrubbed, appears and forms a semicircle behind the object of the surgeon's wrath. All he sees is eyes maintaining direct eye contact with him—just eyes, between the caps and the masks. It works— try it.

Most frequently what I see and must deal with is people who are responding to anger with frustration, passivity, or aggression. I can deal with frustration by asking if my help is needed. I can deal with passivity by giving the person permission to have feelings within a safe environment. I'm going to spend a little more time with anger and aggression.

Anger and Ourselves

One of the things we've done consistently is look at ourselves and how we act in a variety of situations. We're going to do it again. Look at the following diagram.

1. _____

2. _____

3. _____

4. _____

5. _____

Characteristics I'm Proud Of

In each one of the five lines, write one characteristic that you have. A characteristic that helps to define you as a person and a professional. A characteristic you are proud of. I have in mind things like caring, compassionate, fair, responsible, dependable, honest, trustworthy, competent—you get the drift. My five characteristics might look like this:

1.   _caring_ .

2.   _honest_

3.   _competent_

4.   _consistent_

5.   _patient advocate_

Characteristics I'm Proud Of

Now look at the next diagram.

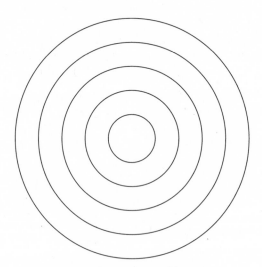

The True Self

If you could only choose one characteristic to describe yourself, which one would it be? Only one. This is the true me. Which one is it? Place the number beside that characteristic in the center of the circles. As the circles go outward, place the other numbers in descending order of importance. That is, the characteristic identified in the center of your circle is the *most* important, the characteristic represented in the next circle going outward is the *next most* important, and so on, until all the characteristics have been represented in these circles.

This is a forced rank order, and I acknowledge that it is difficult to do. My circles might look like this:

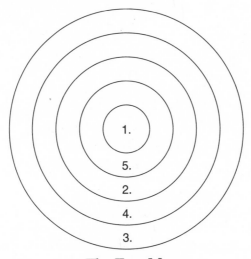

The True Me

The characteristic represented by the number in the center of my circles is my biggest strength. It is also my biggest weakness, and it is where I am most vulnerable to attack by the aggressive person.

Aggressive and manipulative persons are going to know within five minutes of meeting me where I am vulnerable—and I'm not going to have to say, "This is my biggest strength and my biggest weakness." They have an uncanny ability to spot it. I wish I knew how they do that—the truth is, I don't.

We are all, each one of us, *easy targets* of the aggressor. The biggest reason for that is that we really don't want to believe that someone would do that to us. We are inclined to project onto others attributes that we have, and since, as caring professionals, we wouldn't do that, we have trouble believing that someone else *would*. It is important to keep at a conscious level that the aggressive person has no respect for me. I have trouble with that one, too, because I assume that we all respect each other. Oh, boy, am I wrong with some, few people. There really are people out there who are just plain mean. (Even though I understand *why* they're mean, that doesn't give them permission to *be* mean.)

How does the aggressor attack me in my most vulnerable area—my biggest strength. Let's say, for the sake of the discussion, that my biggest strength, the characteristic represented by the number in the center of my circle, is *caring*. The attack might take place something like this:

CASE STUDY

MYTH O'LOGIC HEALTHCARE CENTER: ATTACK OF THE AGGRESSOR

We are in the middle of a staff meeting. Massive changes are due to take place within Myth O'Logic Healthcare Center, and I believe strongly that to facilitate this change I must provide my staff with information, information, information, structure, structure, structure. In keeping with that belief, I'm going over the information I have, including all that I know about outcomes, especially emphasizing quality of care and the important role of nursing, and costs.

Donna raises her hand. I am very conscientious and want my staff to feel free to express their concerns. I believe that Donna must have a concern, and I want to get it out in the open. And I say, "Yes, Donna?" The rest of the interaction goes like this:

Donna: I always thought that you cared about us and about the patients, but I guess I was wrong. All I hear is what *they* want; what *administration* wants. What we have to do to meet *their* bottom line. You give lip service to the quality of patient care, but the real message is dollars. It isn't caring about us and it sure isn't caring about the patients. I was wrong about you.

Well! You could hear a pin drop in the room. I am speechless and so is the rest of the staff. My natural inclination is to rush in (where fools fear to tread) and to defend against that attack. I immediately

MYTH O'LOGIC HEALTHCARE CENTER: ATTACK OF THE
AGGRESSOR Concluded

say, "Oh, yes, I *do* care about you and the patients. Look at all the information I've gotten about our role as nurses, and our contribution
to quality of care. I've knocked myself out to get this information.
It's not fair to accuse me of being uncaring."

And, Donna sits back and folds her arm, smiles to herself, and
thinks, "Gotcha!"

Analysis   Let's diagram this interaction with our parent-adult-
child circles.

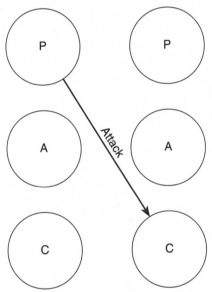

Attack of the Aggressor

Donna is sending a message from her parent to my child—the
seat of my emotions. My thoughts: "She said I didn't *care!* That is
my biggest strength and everybody knows it. It just doesn't make
sense. Why would she say that? If she'd said that sometimes I put
things off to the last minute I'd have understood—because I do.

I'm not very proud of that, but I do. But to say I don't care."

We call it "cognitive dissonance" for the very reason that *it doesn't fit*. It's kind of like a piano that needs tuning. One key is a little off. We know the sound isn't right. It's just that we are not professional tuners and we can't figure out which key it is.

Donna has leveled her attack at my biggest strength. Very deliberately. Because it is also my biggest weakness. Any one of the characteristics I listed will serve as an area of vulnerability—it just depends on which one is the most important to me today. My aggressor can read me like a book.

I think about the movie *Patton* and the scene in which Patton is looking through his field glasses while his tanks demolish Rommel's forces. Patton says, with glee, "Rommel, I read your *?@#&! book." My aggressor can play me like a fiddle.

How in the world do I defend against that while holding to my strongly held belief that I respect myself and the other person (which does not state that I respect the other person's behavior). Assuming that I am prepared to defend myself (ineffective), or that I am speechless (that's OK), what do I do? Here it is—the answer. This is what to do!

Confronting an Aggressive Attack

The first thing I want to do is to *close my mouth* before I start begging for forgiveness for being such a bad person. Then, I want to look Donna straight in the eye and say, calmly and with a sure voice, "I can't respond to that right now. I need a few minutes to gather my thoughts." Say that out loud, with me: *I can't respond to that right now. I need a few minutes to gather my thoughts.* Didn't that feel good?

Donna's message to me, from the parent to the child, effectively stripped me of power, and she did it in a public setting. When I start pleading for forgiveness I acknowledge the transference of power from me to her. This makes the remainder of my staff very uneasy because they have a basic need to know who's in charge? When I say, "I can't respond to that right now. I need a few minutes to gather my thoughts," I take my power back. Look at the diagram of the interaction.

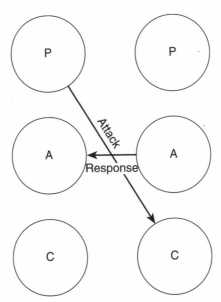

Responding to the Aggressor

I am now in my adult and ready to tackle the problem—adult to adult.

I am going to take those few minutes to mentally construct an assertive message designed to confront Donna with her behavior.

Assertiveness operates under the premise that "each person has the right to be and to express himself or herself, and to feel good (not guilty) about doing so, as long as he or she does not hurt others in the process" (Alberti, Robert E. and Emmons, Michael L. *A Guide to Assertive Living: Your Perfect Right*, 4th ed. San Luis Obispo, CA: Impact Publishers, 1982). It is important to emphasize that while I have the right to express my feelings, I have *no* right to this expression *at the expense of someone else.*

How to Construct an Assertive Message

Many resources are available for learning to be assertive. There are also a few constants in the construction of an assertive message that I find to hold true from expert to expert. These form the basis for an assertive message.

There is also an underlying assumption that the relationship is important. What I am going to do is to attempt to "teach" or "coach" my aggressor to behave in a more acceptable and productive manner—the *sell* level in our leadership model. If the relationship isn't important, this selling job might not work. It's worth a try, though. I might avoid having to drop down to the autocratic *tell*.

The assertive message has three essential parts:

1. I must tell the other person how I feel (feeling).
2. I must tell the other person what made me feel that way (thought).
3. I must tell the other person what I want him or her to do so that I won't feel that way any more (want).

Other guidelines for construction of an assertive message might include a consequence if that *want* is not honored. I consider that to be at the tell level and I choose to redirect by trying to sell the other person on a more effective way of interacting with me. I can always add the fourth part and tell (reprimand) if this doesn't work.

Not only that, if I only have to remember three things, rather than four or five, I am more likely to use them. I have enough to remember without adding a complicated process to my communication skills.

So, I have my three parts: feelings, thought, and want. How do I put those together? First, I must identify the feeling. When Donna attacked me (that was my perception), how did I feel?

To help us out, I have provided a list of "feeling" words. The reason I have done this is that frequently I find that when I say, "How did that make you feel?" the response is often, "Well, I felt that she shouldn't have said that." I would like to offer that that statement is a legitimate thought, even a belief—it is not a *feeling*. Here are the feeling words:

Feeling Words

Angry	Sad	Happy
Sorry	Frustrate	Guilty

Feeling Words (Continued)

Embarrassed	Joyous	Disappointed
Great	Tired	Rejected
Warm	Numb	Good
Defensive	Diminished	Screwed
Unsupported	Weary	Raped
Loved	Appreciated	Manipulated
Taken advantage of	Failure	Exhausted
Refreshed	Accepted	Dumb
Incompetent	Depressed	Bored
Hurt	Anxious	Intimidated
Lonely	Afraid	Furious

This list of feeling words is not meant to be all-inclusive, or exclusive. It is just an example of what I mean when I say, "How did that make you feel?"

Now I am ready to construct my assertive message, designed to confront Donna with the impact her behavior has on me, and what I want her to do about it.

My thinking will go like this:

I feel . . .
When (thought) . . .
I want . . .

How did I feel when Donna accused me of not caring? I felt *awful*. I felt *defensive*. I felt *attacked*. I felt *furious*. I felt *exhausted*. I felt *embarrassed*. Any others that you can think of that you might feel under similar circumstances? Write 'em down.

Next I must identify what made me feel that way, and it might sound like this:

When you accuse me of not caring . . .

Then I must tell her what I want her to do in the future to assure that I don't feel this way again; and it might sound something like this:

I want you to bring your criticisms of me to a private meeting—not a public one.

There! That's a classic assertive message:

Assertive Message "A"

I feel defensive, attacked, furious, and embarrassed
when you accuse me in a public setting of not caring.
In the future, when you have criticisms of a personal nature, **I
want** you to tell me in a private setting.

It's all out there. Nothing is left to the imagination. This is frequently called an "I message." It's good. All the parts are there: I feel; when; I want. *Now let's make it better.*

We're going to work magic with the classic assertive message: *We're going to take the dreaded word "you" out of it.* Rather than saying, "When you . . . ," I'm going to state what I see and I hear that has made me so unhappy. And, this is how it will look and sound.

Assertive Message "B"

I feel defensive, attacked, and furious
when I hear that I am not a caring person. It is especially embarrassing to hear that in a public setting.
In the future, **I want** to hear any personal criticisms in a private setting.

Now, compare and contrast the two assertive messages. Which one is stronger? "B" is stronger! Why? *Because we kept our personal power.* The minute I say that I feel a certain way because of something "you" said or did, I have given you power over me. I am saying that I am powerless in the face of your accusations, and I am not powerless. *I refuse* to relinquish my personal power to Donna.

Another benefit I derive from keeping the message in the "I" is that I give to Donna the same thing that I said I wanted, and that's "wiggle room." Because Donna can now say, "I didn't accuse you of not caring. I just meant . . ." And, I can say, "Good, because I don't like it when I hear that I'm not a caring person, especially in a public setting." Then turn loose—let it go.

I must remember that my goal is to change her behavior,

not to rub her nose in it. In fact, to make her grovel would be counter to my belief that all persons are entitled to respect. *Stay focused.*

"You" Is a Four-Letter Word!

I am firmly convinced that if I can limit the number of times I use the "you" word, I'll be far more effective in my interactions with others. I want to use "you" when I have something positive to say. I want to say "I" when I am addressing the impact of someone else's behavior on me. This is what I *want* to do, and what I *will* do when I have a choice. If, however, the other person chooses not to respond positively to this teaching, this coaching, then I will use the "you" word. I have the authority to be authoritarian; I would rather lead than direct. It is a way of keeping the ball in the other person's court. Donna is in charge of whether I stay at sell or drop down to tell.

Let's do one more assertive message.

Let's proceed to a situation in which I have already spoken to the other person about her behavior and she has ignored me.

Lucille is a clinical nurse specialist who reports to me in our decentralized management plan. We are completely reorganizing the maternal-child program to effect an earlier discharge. I have asked her to orient the nursing staff to the first of several critical paths that will be the organizing framework for patient care. We have built in an intensive patient-education focus, and followup after discharge. Lucille has not done this. We have already had one conversation about my expectations and her responsibilities.

In our second meeting, Lucille informs me that staff development is not her job. She is a case manager. My initial reaction is:

Assertive Message "C"

(Feeling) I feel p*ssed and exhausted
(Thought) when you deliberately defy me.
(Want) I would appreciate it if you would do what I ask you to do.

Yep. I used the p*ssed word. I want the strongest word I need in order to get the message across to the other person——and no stronger. P*ssed is the worst word that I know that I use, and I use it rarely. And when I do people perk up—*uh-oh, Katie used the p*ss word.* I know worse words, I just don't use them. (Slight digression: I hear young people talking today, on the streets and on television, and every other word is the F-word. I am offended by its use; hearing it serves to pollute the air around me. The word, however, no longer shocks me. It has no meaning. It's wasted. Many teenagers today don't even know how to insult each other—they have no language skills.) Because I rarely use strong language, the shock value has an effect on Lucille.

Again, I have the "you" word in there because that's the way I'm used to thinking. Let's take it out and replace it with "I" and see how it sounds.

Assertive Message "D"

> I feel angry and exhausted
> When I hear "No" in response to a direct order.
> I want my directives followed when given.
> (Consequence) I will consider failure to follow my directive to be insubordination.

Again, I have been very direct and very clear about what has happened, how I feel about it, what I want to have happen, and I've added the consequence if my directive is not followed. At the same time I have still allowed Lucille wiggle room. She still has room to say, "I wasn't defying you. I'm just not through working on the lesson plan for the in-service." And I can say, "Good. I expect it to be complete and ready to implement in one week."

And, I haven't said she is a bad person. I have said nothing designed to make Lucille defensive—to have to defend her integrity. It is not my goal to put her down. It is my goal to *change her behavior.*

The Beginner with Assertiveness

The beginner with assertiveness is going to require more than a few minutes to construct an assertive message because it hasn't been our usual pattern of communication. That's OK. I suggest the following steps as part of the learning curve we all experience when we're doing something for the first time:

1. Give myself time to get my thoughts in order. Rather than saying, "I need a few minutes to gather my thoughts," I'll say, "I can't respond to that right now. We'll meet in my office tomorrow morning to discuss this."

2. Go to my office, or home; take a piece of 8½ by 11 paper and write on it:

   I feel

   I think

   I want

3. Write down every feeling that I can think of that welled up during this confrontation—every one. Chances are that what I want to say won't be the first word that comes to mind; it will appear during the process.

4. Then write down what the other person did that made me feel that way. It will probably appear as ". . . when she or you did something. *That's OK.* The important thing is to get the action down—not how we say it—not yet.

5. Write down what I want that person to do in the future. It will probably be *she* or *you* and *that's OK.* I want to get the thought down just the way it comes to mind.

6. *Now we work the magic and take the "you" and "she" out of it.*

Postscript

I am often asked if I would really tell someone that I was intimidated. Yes, I would—in a heartbeat. Why would I do that? Because intimidation is being used as a weapon. When I acknowledge the intimidation, it no longer exists as a weapon. Now what is the other person going to do?

It also isn't necessary to say, "I feel intimidated . . ." I can say, "It intimidates me when . . ." The important thing is to use the emotion-laden word.

I'm also a great believer in the "Sunshine Law." If it's out on the table then I can deal with it better. Intimidation exposed to the sunshine loses its strength. This is consistent with my belief that hidden agendas are destructive. What you see is what you get. I told you in the beginning who I was, what I expected of you, and what you could expect of me. I am consistent.

Warning: Sometimes people who are passive by habit, upon learning assertiveness skills, become holy terrors—they go overboard. Be patient. We need to feel a level of comfort with new skills before we can practice moderation.

Sometimes people who are aggressive by habit, upon attending an assertiveness class become too passive and fearful of saying *anything*. Be patient. We need to feel a level of comfort with new skills before we can practice moderation.

Our method of assertiveness, by keeping it in the "I," is a kind and gentle way to confront unwanted behavior. We demonstrate that we truly care about the other person, at the same time that we maintain respect for ourselves.

Now! Go and be assertive. You can do it!

Let's move on and talk about manipulation.

MANIPULATION

Let's just get one thing straight. *We all manipulate.* Look at all the courses we can take to teach us how to "close a sale," "negotiate," or the grandaddy of all such courses, Dale Carnegie's *How to Win Friends and Influence People.* Do my grandsons manipulate me with their raves about my deviled eggs?

We aren't talking about everyday people-stuff manipulation. We're talking about manipulation that says that my needs as a person are totally irrelevant—we're talking about manipulation that is destructive to the relationship.

The Great Manipulator truly has a lot in common with the aggressive person. Both are very narcissistic and self-centered. Neither one cares a hoot about you and me. The manipulator professes caring. Manipulators cry wonderful crocodile tears. Their actions, however, speak far louder than words. What they care about is themselves—not the healthy caring about self that we are attempting to foster. It is an unhealthy caring that discounts the value of the other person.

We have identified anger as the basic, underlying reason for aggression—that act of lashing out at some ill-defined other whose fault it is that the angry person is experiencing such anguish. Add to that anger a lack of trust and we have the great manipulator. The manipulator doesn't trust that we will be there when we are needed.

The manipulative person has problems with trust that date back to early childhood. Remember Erickson's growth and development task of trust versus mistrust? The manipulative person simply never did master that task.

That implies that if Mom had done a better job of instilling trust in the baby, then we wouldn't be faced with this manipulator today. I think moms get a bad rap on this one. In fact, I think some kids come our of the chute that way. If I talk to any nurse who has one or more years experience in a *normal* newborn nursery, she'll tell me that she can pick them out. "This one is going to cause problems. That one is going to cause problems." It's typically babies who underreact, without observable cause; or babies who overreact to stimuli that don't seem to faze the baby in the next bassinet. The nurse can't tell you if the baby is going to grow up to be a serial killer; she *can* tell you which ones are going to have problems. I would love to do a 20-year longitudinal study and test that belief. I'll take a random assignment of any registered nurse who has had at least one year's experience in a normal newborn nursery. I *know* their predictions would hold up.

I don't think the mom *can* meet that baby's trust needs. I think the baby is wired differently. I think that about the time Mom thinks she has it made and has connected with this baby, the baby moves a half inch, as if to say, "You're not going to be able to pin me down." This baby grows up, and is now one of the 20 percent of my staff who create 80 percent of my problems.

What we truly must understand about the manipulator is that she (at less than a conscious level) lives in holy terror of having a need that won't be met; that when she needs us, we won't be there. She has dependency needs that I couldn't meet if I lived to be 124 and devoted 63 hours a day to her and her alone—*it's never enough.* That must be pretty scary. It scares the heck out of me that but for the grace of God, I could have been that way.

The manipulator, therefore, must (1) constantly keep us "hooked" into rescuing her, and (2) constantly "test" us in order to reassure herself that she can depend on us, that we do mean what we say. Let's take a look and see how this works.

You and I live in a rather abstract world, when we stop to think about it. It really is not all black and white—it's tinged with gray. And, there are very few absolutes. Mostly we live in a world surrounded by a dotted line, to indicate that the border is flexible to accommodate differing circumstances. (A temperature of 102 degrees F while serious enough to require attention, is not *too* serious when it occurs in a normally robust child. It can be devastating to someone who is 75 years old and frail.)

My manipulator lives in a black and white, very concrete world, surrounded by a heavy, solid line.

Story: I have a thing about cleanliness with people who are providing direct patient care—because of what it says to the patient. This includes shoes in addition to the clothing. I'm delighted that nurses can now wear Reeboks or Nikes or any other shoe built for comfort. I want them *clean*, and I emphasize this in my orientation meetings. I've been known to require people to clock out, go polish shoes, clock in, and return the polish to me to emphasize that I mean what I say. Now, you and I know what I mean by cleanliness, don't we? We even understand clean shoes even though it's an abstract concept. The manipulator can't handle abstract concepts like clean, neat, fair. My manipulator is going to say, "What do you mean by clean?" I must be prepared to describe "clean" in clearly understood, operational terms. So, I draw a diagram.

Good day—2 smudges

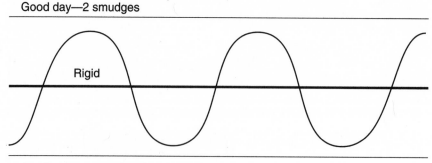

Bad day—0 smudges

Making an Abstract Concept Concrete

And, I say, " Do you see this line in the middle? That's rigid. I'm not rigid. I have a range from good to bad.

"See this upper line? That defines a good day. On a good day,

and I define a good day as one in which the census is at 80 percent—maybe 90 percent—the case mix is within the standards established for this unit, I have a full staff, the budget has been sub-
mitted and approved, and there are no pressures beyond the
day-to-day functioning of the unit. On a good day, I can tolerate
two smudges on your shoes.

"See this bottom line? That defines a bad day. A bad day is
when the census is 110 percent, I am short-staffed due to blizzard
conditions, any other natural disaster, or a flu epidemic, and I'm
under pressure to cut costs in my budget, which is due next week.
That's a bad day. On a bad day, I suggest that you live at the foot
of the cross—no smudges—none." (Note that I'm not talking about
a "bad hair day" because I don't think I have a right to bring that
to work—I have an obligation to leave that at the door when I walk
in.)

That's pretty concrete, isn't it?

My manipulator, let's have it be a man, and let's call him
William, isn't going to try me on a bad day. That would be dumb,
and manipulators are not dumb. He is going to test me on a good
day. He will come to work with three smudges on his shoes (the
standard is no more than two). I notice it and take him into my office for a consultation on this violation of standards. The interaction goes something like this:

Me: I see three smudges on those shoes in violation of
standards that are very important to me. We discussed those
standards and you agreed to adhere to them. Here is the
shoe polish. Clock out, polish your shoes, clock back in, and
return the shoe polish to me.

William: I can't believe you're doing this. Who's always
there for you? Who gets most of the cards and letters from
patients filled with appreciation for the excellent patient care
they received? Who volunteers to work overtime when
we're in a crunch? Who volunteers to serve on committees?
Who do you call on when you're in a bind? And you're
going to make me clock out and polish my shoes? I can't
believe this!

Me: (Oh, no! He's right! He does provide excellent patient
care. [Recall that two of my characteristic strengths, reflected
in my "circle," are "caring," and "patient advocate."] Why

am I criticizing him for smudges on his shoes when he is so dependable? He's right. It looks like I don't care anything about him—just his stupid shoes. I'm being unreasonable. Patient care is why we're here.) "You're right. I appreciate what you're doing, especially your devotion to quality of care for the patients. I'll let the shoe thing slide this time, but don't do it again."

What Did Katie Accomplish?

I didn't accomplish anything productive! All I did was to establish a new boundary, a new standard. Now the acceptable standard for dirty shoes is *three* smudges. Because the next time I call William in to discuss dirty shoes he's going to say, "Why do I have to go polish my shoes for three smudges? I had three smudges two weeks ago and it was ok. What has changed? I have trouble abiding by rules when I don't know what the rules are—when they change from day to day. What is it that you want? I just don't understand women."

And my strengths in my "consistency" and "dependability" were just challenged. And, I wonder, "What happened? Where did I lose control (of the agenda)?"

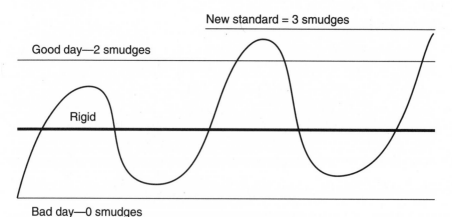

Changing the Standard

Analysis   The manipulator's strength lies in his being able to control the agenda. That's exactly what William did. We started out talking about standards of cleanliness and moved very quickly to discussing his quality of patient care, his willingness to participate in the unit's team efforts, and his willingness to go the extra mile during times of need. These are separate issues! The one is not even vaguely related to the other. Not only that, he is citing behavior I expect of all my staff. Somehow William made it sound so extraordinary that he deserved special consideration.

How did I get caught up in playing this game? I started out being the *initiator* and changed positions to become the *responder*. I quickly became defensive. Let's diagram that interaction on our parent-adult-child circles and see what happened.

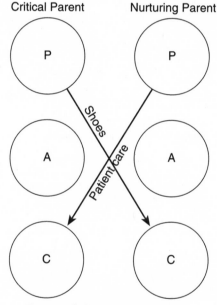

Crossed Communication

What Am I To Do?

Set limits and stay focused   I am doing the manipulator no favor by bending the rules, regardless of the reason. I am actually contributing to his sense of insecurity, his feeling that he can't trust me, his belief that I won't be there when he needs me. Now his level of tension and anxiety is going to be so high that he'll have to

do something else to "test the limits." Lord only knows what it's
going to be next time.

The only thing that I can safely predict is that it will be on a
"good day."

Recommended Strategy

I recommend writing down the topic, or issue, I want to address on a three-by-five or four-by-six card, in big, black, box letters. I place this card on the desk in front of me and look at it often
during the interaction. That way, when William starts talking
about his excellence in patient care, and his loyalty and dependability, I can look down at the card and see DIRTY SHOES. And I can
say to William, "I appreciate your excellence in patient care, your
loyalty, and your dependability. Thank you for that. The topic
today is dirty shoes."

The manipulator is also good at avoiding having to deal with
problems because he is so highly skilled at giving them to us! Look
at this diagram.

My behavior unacceptable to others   Other person owns the problem   Effective strategy: listener, counselor
No–problem zone   or   Both persons own problem
Other person's behavior unacceptable to me   I own the problem   Effective strategy: assertiveness

Monkey on the Back

This is called the Monkey on the Back, or Who Owns the
Problem. The basic premise is that I already have as many mon-

keys (problems) as I can handle and don't want to take any more in to raise, given the care and feeding that monkeys demand. The idea is to avoid "buying" the other person's monkeys, or problems.

When my behavior is unacceptable to others, the other person owns the problem (I set limits on how dirty William's shoes could be; this constituted a problem for William). The correct action for me to take is to be a listener/counselor/conflict manager. (I listen to and acknowledge his excellence in patient care— however, I do not buy his problem. I keep the monkey on his back.)

> Fool me once, shame on you. Fool me twice, shame on me.
>
> —Gomer Pyle

When the other person's behavior is unacceptable to me I own the problem, and the correct action for me to take is to be assertive and to state the problem and what I want to have done about it (I set limits on how dirty William's shoes could be; I stated my problem and what I wanted done about it).

In the middle of the diagram we have a common zone, in which we (1) both own the problem, or (2) neither one of us has a problem.

The manipulator, like William will attempt to at least push the problem into the center—and he was successful, wasn't he?

The Victim

Sometimes people are truly victimized by other people or by circumstances. We want to rescue because we're caring people—it's almost second nature with us. That's OK on a temporary basis to make it through the crisis, but then we must back off and allow the person who has been victimized to make his own decisions, take his own actions, and be responsible for the consequences.

> Oh, what a tangled web we weave When first we practice to deceive.
>
> —Sir Walter Scott

Interestingly, true victims want help in resolving the presenting problem; they don't want to be continuously rescued. When we continue to rescue the victim we make the victim dependent on us, and the victim begins to hate us for it.

Manipulators, however, often claim victim status (even though they, individually, have not been victimized by me) in order to gain the upper hand in the relationship. The victim role is very powerful, and the person who employs this strategy is not going to give it up easily.

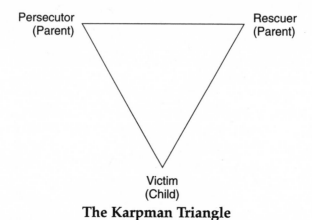

The Karpman Triangle

This is the Karpman triangle, heavily used by the parent-adult-child folks, and it illustrates beautifully how the manipulator attempts to put the monkey (problem) on my back through use of the role of the victim.

1. I counsel with William about his dirty shoes (persecutor to victim).
2. William tells me how good he is (excellence in patient care, etc.) (victim to rescuer).
3. I rush in to tell William that he is right. He's a very good person and I shouldn't be complaining about his shoes (rescuer to victim).
4. William says that I should have been more appreciative of his contributions to patient care (persecutor to victim).
5. I say that he is right—I forgot for a moment what was important (victim to rescuer).

6. William says, why don't we just forget it ever happened (rescuer to victim)?

Let's plot William's and my interaction on the Karpman triangle to see how it doesn't go anywhere and is completely under William's control.

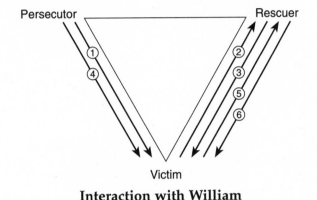

Interaction with William

William successfully manipulated a role change. He started out as the victim and quickly cast me in the victim role begging the rescuer for forgiveness.

What strikes me as important in this exchange is that each one of the participants is assuming either the parent or the child role. What I want you to do is to draw a dotted line across the middle of that triangle, and write ADULT on it. Just like this.

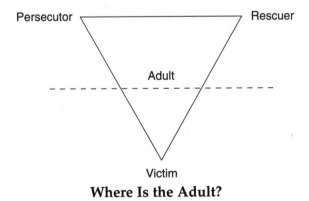

Where Is the Adult?

When I see one of these exchanges beginning to take place, I'm going to get into my adult fast and stop it! My only prayer is to stay in my adult because if I don't stay in my adult, the manipulator will keep me running around that triangle and I'll never resolve *any* issue.

The Extremes to Which Manipulators Go

Manipulators are very good at what they do and are convinced that we are easy marks. By and large they are right. Nurses are professional rescuers (we mentioned that once before). Manipulators depend on that. If we are not easy, as with William's shoes, the manipulator is prepared to pull out all the stops—all's fair in love or war, and this is war.

I must be prepared to hear and to respond to:

"Joe's shoes are just as dirty as mine. Why aren't you talking to him?"

"It's a cultural thing. In my culture clean shoes are not important. You're criticizing my culture."

"The only reason you're talking about shoes is that you don't want to talk about what's really bothering you—that I have more education than you do and you're jealous that I know more than you do."

"I live in the projects. It isn't fair to pick on me. I can't afford shoe polish."

"It must be hard to be an older nurse in today's changing world."

"You're a racist (because I'm black, white, yellow, brown, etc.)."

"I'm a single mom and it's hard enough to just get to work. I shouldn't be expected to live up to the same standards as everyone else."

"It's my lifestyle. I'm a lesbian and you don't approve."

You know what I say to that one? "I didn't hire you to have sex with you. The topic is dirty shoes."

I must be prepared for hot-button issues guaranteed to put me on the defensive. The purpose is to change the agenda—to get me off my issue and onto his.

Note: The manipulator truly cannot help being manipulative.

That does not mean that it's OK. We must not support that behavior by being wishy-washy with our expectations. When we are firm, fair, caring, and consistent, even in the face of a master manipulator, *we are being kind in our own gentle way.*

I also don't have victims on my staff. If the person wants to be a victim the 16 hours a day she's not working for me, she is entitled to do that. My staff is composed of adults who are empowered to make their own decisions and are held accountable for their actions. I will not "dumb down" nursing to accommodate a manipulator.

Summary of Helpful Hints

- Anger is part of the "fight-or-flight" reaction to a perceived threat to self.
- Anger includes the element of *resentment.*
- The five ways of responding to anger, from the most constructive to the most destructive, are: assertiveness, frustration, passivity, aggression, and rage.
- The assertive message has three essential parts: I feel, I think, and I want.
- Assistance with frustration is most easily accomplished by using active listening skills within an assertive message.
- Passivity is a nonproductive way of dealing with anger. However, it might be the person's only way of coping. Use of active listening skills to give the person permission to express feelings is an effective and appropriate action.
- The aggressive person does not care about us, our right, or our feeling. Confrontation of an aggressive person is done by listening to feelings and responding to facts with an assertive message.
- Think safety, gentle, firm, slow, and easy when dealing with the person in a state of rage.
- Be firm, fair, caring, and consistent with the manipulative person.

We have consistently applied several of our supporting principles while dealing with difficult people:

Principle 2: Interaction with others is more effective when we meet them where they are rather than where we want them to be.

Principle 4: We can't change anyone's behavior but our own.

Principle 6: Communication is most effective when the speaker and the audience speak the same language.

Principle 7: Most people who are difficult to deal with are responding to their own anger or fear.

Conflict resolution can be even more complex—especially when *two* people are being difficult. We'll apply everything we've learned to this point plus a little bit more as we tackle conflict resolution in our final chapter. We're almost done!

8 CHAPTER

Conflict Resolution

When the Irresistible Force Meets the Immovable Object

Many managers believe that the presence of conflict on the unit, or in the facility or agency, is a sign of management failure. *False belief!* A little conflict can be healthy. In fact, *June Bowman and *Mary Lou Jones believe strongly that, "Without conflict, there is no growth."

Conflicts can occur (1)within individuals, (2) between individuals, or (3) between an individual and the organization. (This list is not meant to be exclusive.)

The conflicts that most tax our skills and sensibilities as nurse managers are those between members of our staff. We frequently call these conflicts "personality clashes." My preference is that these conflicts take care of themselves without my intervention. It's when the conflict creates an unhealthy tension that is *not* being resolved that I must intervene, as a manager and a leader.

WHAT IS A CONFLICT AND WHERE DOES IT COME FROM?

Conflict is, very simply, a clash between two opposing forces. That's too simple, however, because the conflict can be between two positive forces, two negative forces, one positive and one

negative force, or two positive-negative forces. Let's look at each
one.

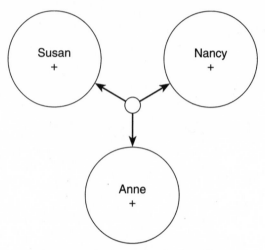

Approach-Approach Conflict

This illustrates the pull we feel when we have to make a
choice between equally desirable goals. I have three sisters: Susan,
Nancy, and Anne. I have been invited to each one of their homes
for a special occasion on the same day. Each invitation is appeal-
ing. Which one do I choose? I am torn. This is a *conflict*.

At a professional level, perhaps I have just been offered the
opportunity to add one of two excellent nurses to my staff. I have
had experience with both and they are both desirable. Each one
has strengths I desperately need.

How do I decide? This is called *approach-approach*. While all
conflict generates some anxiety, this is the least anxiety producing.
We would like all of our conflicts to be approach-approach.

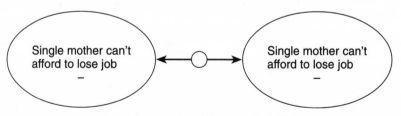

Avoidance-Avoidance Conflict

Have you heard the old western saying, "Would you rather be hung for a sheep or a goat?" That's what this diagram illustrates. I'm hung either way—neither option is desirable. Let's say that I must eliminate one position. The newest person, when I think of seniority, is a single mother just out of school who needs this job desperately and is a good, solid nurse who learns new skills daily. The other nurse who is learning new skills daily is also a single mother just out of school who needs this job desperately. There is no decision without pain; neither decision is desirable. This is called *avoidance-avoidance* and it produces a high level of anxiety.

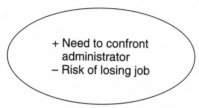

+ Need to confront
administrator
– Risk of losing job

Approach-Avoidance Conflict

A third kind of conflict is *approach-avoidance*. We're probably very familiar with this one. Should I or shouldn't I? I can see a positive benefit and a negative consequence to any decision I make. I want to confront my administrator about my perception that the expectations as stated in my job description are excessive and unattainable (approach). At the same time I know that when I do that I am going to risk losing my job (avoidance). Which choice do I make? What I really want is to achieve my goal and avoid the chance of losing my job. I can't have it both ways. Some anxiety accompanies this conflict.

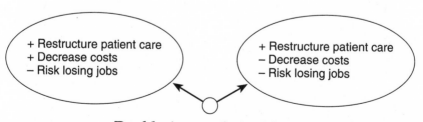

+ Restructure patient care
+ Decrease costs
– Risk losing jobs

+ Restructure patient care
– Decrease costs
– Risk losing jobs

Double Approach-Avoidance

The fourth, and most complex of the conflicts, is *double approach-avoidance*. This is where I can see the positive and negative aspects of *each one* of the alternatives. For example: My agency is undergoing consultation for reengineering and I have been asked to submit suggestions for my area of responsibility. I submit two plans: (1) implement patient focused care with an emphasis on ancillary staff who are cross-trained, and (2) implement patient-focused care with an emphasis on case management. Both plans have strengths and weaknesses. I am truly ambivalent and am likely to experience a high level of anxiety.

Personality Clashes

The conflicts that develop between two staff persons usually arise because of a clash between two strong persons, each one of whom might have high control needs and sees the other person as frustrating that need. The need can represent a basic value; for example, one nurse values life at any cost; the other nurse believes in "letting go." Or, the conflict can be between two departments, each one of which wants to be "in charge" (control needs again).

When they negotiate between themselves for shared power, there is no reason for us to be involved. It is when the power struggle escalates to the point that it is affecting patient care or the ease with which the unit is functioning that we must intervene. When the parties continue to jab at each other, they are really exhibiting an approach-avoidance type of conflict. They are *approaching* each other in the quest for power; at the same time they are *avoiding* dealing with the power issue directly.

Resolving conflicts is going to require me to apply all of my knowledge of motivation, behavior modification, communication, and methods of resolving conflicts.

Conflict Resolution

There are five ways of resolving conflicts:

1. Collaboration
2. Compromise

3. Competition
4. Avoidance
5. Accommodation

(Anastasi, Tom. *Conflict without Casualty: Personality Negotiating.* New York: Sterling Publishing Co., 1993; Briles, Judith. *The Briles Report on Women in Healthcare.* San Francisco: Jossey-Bass, 1994).

Let's look at the strengths and weaknesses in each one of these methods.

Collaboration: Win-Win

This is the conflict-resolution equivalent of assertiveness. Each person respects the other person as well as self. Each is willing to speak up and to say this is what I want, and is also willing to listen to what the other person wants. This method is most effective when the two parties have an interdependent relationship. It is a method of conflict resolution within which each party leaves the confrontation with a belief that she gained more than she had to give up. The result of a collaboration is likely to be a long-term improvement in the relationship.

Compromise: Win/Lose–Win/Lose

We're having to give something up in order to reach a resolution to the conflict. Each person has a sense of loss. We might have to do this because of expediency or time constraints. However, the basic conflict has not been resolved and will resurface at another time. There might be a sense that this is "better than nothing." Compromise, as a short-term solution, is often used to buy time until the air clears enough to allow for collaboration.

Competition: Win-Lose

The purpose of competition is for getting my way and implies a power play. It forces the other person to submit to my demands; it also alienates the other person. If I have a big stake in getting my way I might want to compete, especially if I believe I don't have anything to lose. This is definitely not the method of conflict resolution that I want to use with my superior—unless I had termination in mind!

Avoidance: Ignore It and It Will Go Away

Sometimes the best action to take is no action. Avoidance doesn't necessarily mean that I am running away from an issue; it means that sometimes conflicts resolve themselves if I ignore them or leave them alone. And, sometimes it is prudent to put a problem on hold for a brief period of time. There might be a need for a "cooling off period." I might need time for the creaky wheels of the bureaucracy to work. I might also be aware that I'm dealing with a very complex situation that does not lend itself to conflict resolution at this time. I also use avoidance when I have applied expectancy theory and have decided that "it isn't worth it."

The conflict is still there, and those that do not resolve themselves through application of "benign neglect" will resurface. However, I have bought time to think about it and to formulate a strategy more in keeping with the win-win goals of collaboration.

Accommodation: Lose-Win

Accommodation is analogous to the passive method of dealing with anger. The accommodator likes to help, and usually conforms easily. It is an effective means of dealing with conflict when the goal is not important or when I have decided that I am in a no-win situation. In other words, I want to keep the peace, value the relationship over the issue, have little or no power, or I value being a team player. It is definitely the method I want to use when I evaluate the situation and determine that there is no way I could win—even in a collaborative win-win mode.

The issue will more than likely rear its ugly head at a future date when I choose to accommodate.

Method of Choice

The preferred method of choice for effective conflict resolution is *win-win*, or *collaboration*. This is the strategy that we want to use to bring about a "cease-fire" between two persons who are at war with each other.

THE CONFLICT-RESOLUTION PROCESS

There really is a process, or steps we can take, that will help us apply the collaborative method of conflict resolution to a personality clash between two persons (or two departments—the process is the same). Here it is, adapted from J. Crawley, *Constructive Conflict Management*, (San Diego: Pfeiffer and Company, 1992).

First: Take an Impartial Approach

I have time and again said that the first thing I have to do is to look at myself. I have to do it again.

I must ask myself: Am I impartial? What is my perception of this conflict? Do I believe that Pat is right and Becky is wrong? If I do, *I cannot participate in this process.* My body language alone would give me away, and I would effectively set Pat and Becky up for failure; it wouldn't be fair to them. If I am partial, my obligation to Pat and Becky is to call in someone from the outside: from human resources, a social worker, a psych nurse who has the skills, or a psychologist. If, however, I am truly impartial, then I can facilitate this process. I *must:*

- Maintain and communicate respect.

Second: Maintain a Sensitive and Authoritative Approach

I must begin this process by establishing the ground rules. I must be very clear about my expectations: what I expect of the participants and what they can expect of me.

I intend to maintain vigorous control of the *process,* not the *people.* And, I must keep uppermost in my mind that my goal is that there is something in the resolution for each person (win-win).

I must stay very focused on the present and on the goal.

- Set ground rules.
- Create a safe environment within which the participants feel free to express their feelings to each other and to me.

Third: Focus on Behavior

We've said this throughout the book. What I want to focus on, and what I want the participants to focus on, is what I can "see" and "hear." I don't want to hear, "She's an uppity b****." I want to hear what the person sees or hears that leads her to that conclusion.

I'm going to use skills I learned from the parent-adult-child model, along with active-listening skills, to keep the participants focused *on the issues,* not on the persons.

I'll start with open-ended questions to start the process, then I'll focus on more specific information.

Fourth: Get Information Quickly

Do you remember when you were studying for state boards and your instructor told you to mark the first response that came to your mind—and to not go back and correct it (because it is likely that you would make a mistake). The reason I want to get the information quickly is related to that. I might say, "OK, you two, I've had enough of this bickering. Both of you come to my office tomorrow morning at 8:00 sharp. We're going to take care of this." What I will have accomplished is that Pat and Becky are going to go to their respective homes after work and stew and think, "Uh-oh. What am I going to say? I don't want to say—in front of Katie." Each one will begin running away from the issue and trying to find something to hide behind—and I won't have a *collaborative* resolution to the conflict. I'll have *avoidance* or *accommodation.*

I'll really have to use my listening skills to avoid being sidetracked and my assertiveness skills to keep them on track.

Fifth: Identify Differences

I may think that I already know what the problem is. I must resist the temptation to share this great and glorious knowledge with Pat and Becky. They're going to have to do it *themselves!*

I'm going to ask closed questions designed to elicit specific information. Questions such as, "What does Becky do that is driving you crazy?"

Sixth: Work on Areas of Improvement

Now I'm going to ask open-ended questions to generate options for what would make life better. I will establish the boundaries beyond which the participants cannot go with their options for improvement, and will also ensure that the options are very specific.

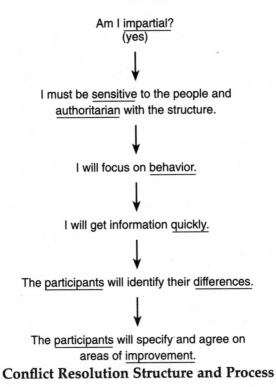

Am I impartial?
(yes)

I must be sensitive to the people and
authoritarian with the structure.

I will focus on behavior.

I will get information quickly.

The participants will identify their differences.

The participants will specify and agree on
areas of improvement.

Conflict Resolution Structure and Process

Let's move on and see how this process works with Pat and Becky.

PAT AND BECKY
A One-Act Play about Conflict Resolution
Written, Produced, and Directed
by
Katie O'Sullivan Mott

The Play: Tense, taut drama about opposing forces in a healthcare setting, played out by the two participants and resolved by taking advantage of the able skills of the nurse manager. A one-act play. Members of the Cast:

Becky T., nurse's aide who rushes through her patient care and has begun to spend the rest of her time at the desk, barking orders to the other staff, patients, and family members.

Pat C., an experienced nurse who provides excellent patient care, but has begun to withdraw and is not communicating with her peers.

You, the nurse manager who is learning how to resolve conflicts between two staff members.

Commentator, an off-stage presence who comments on the interactions.

The Action:

At the Nurses' Station
(Stage Directions)

Pat C., without warning, very quietly tells **Becky T.** that if she tells her what to do one more time she'll throw charts all over the nurses' station, scream at the top of her lungs, and see to it that everyone in the place comes running to see what's wrong.

> (Dialogue)
> **Becky T.** (loudly, and with anger): If you'd do what needs to be done around here I wouldn't have to tell you what to do.

Commentator: You were neutral, maintained respect, communicated your intentions, set ground rules, and asked an open-ended question designed to start the process. You stayed in your "adult," and were assertive.

(Stage Directions)

You are standing close by and hear the words and sense the strong feelings.

(Dialogue)

You (addressing both Pat and Becky): It really distresses me [feeling] when I see this argument in such a public place [thought]. Come with me to my office [any private place] and let's talk [want].

(In the Office)

You: I can see that you are having a hard time working together. To be sure that I truly understand the difficulty, I want both of you to understand that I will listen to each one of you, individually, and ask that you do not interrupt each other. It is important for you to be honest with each other, and with me, and also that you respect each other when you're making your comments. After each one of you has told me what is making you so unhappy, we'll talk about what needs to change, and whether you can make those changes. Do you understand? First, you, Becky. What are you unhappy about?

Becky (loudly, with anger): She drives me crazy with just walking around and not saying anything to anybody. It's like the rest of us don't count.

You: Could you be more specific? Tell me one thing that Pat does that makes you so unhappy?

Becky (still angry): She never

Commentator: You were assertive in stating your request for information from Becky. And, you used your active listening skills to reflect her feelings while you stayed focused on the facts and in control. Becky felt that you had really heard her.

helps out around the nurses' station. She thinks when she takes care of *her* patients that's all there is to do. There are still lights to answer, the telephone to answer, charts to get for doctors, and 50 bazillion other things to do, especially when someone else is at lunch or on break. I can't do it all by myself.

You: Sounds like you're feeling taken advantage of because you don't think Pat is carrying her load.

Becky: That's exactly right.

You: Pat, I'd like to hear about your difficulties with Becky.

Pat (angrily): I just can't stand being around her. She bosses me around like I'm an incompetent know-nothing and I don't like it. I know what my job is and I do it. Just because I don't talk and laugh a lot and hang around the nurses' station she thinks I'm not doing anything. I probably answer more lights than anyone on the unit. Besides, she doesn't have any right to tell me what to do.

You: Am I right in thinking that you feel that your work is not appreciated, and that you resent getting told what to do by someone who has a lower position than you?

Pat: I *don't* think my work is appreciated. I didn't mean to sound like I thought I was more important than Becky—it *did* sound that way. What I'm trying to say is that I mind being told what to do at *all*, by *anyone* since I am doing a good job and

Commentator: You reflected Pat's feelings of not being appreciated, and focused on the specific behavior that caused those feelings. You stayed in your adult and accepted Pat's perception of the problem; you asked closed questions to check the accuracy of your perceptions, and you got information quickly.

Commentator: "You have identified the differences between Pat and Becky and have begun to work on areas of improvement by maintaining control of the process, using open-ended questions to generate options, and asking for specific suggestions."

carrying more than my load of extra responsibility. Becky thinks that because I'm not noisy about doing extra work that I'm not working. It isn't true; I *am* working.

You: So, you're saying that you are more than pulling your load without being told what to do, and that your contributions to the unit are not recognized?

Pat: Right.

You: I want to be sure that I understand the issues. Becky, you feel responsible for the general unit work in addition to your patient care obligations, and you believe that Pat wouldn't pull her fair share of the load if you didn't step in and take charge. Is that accurate?

Becky: Yes!

You: Pat, you believe that you are carrying more than your share of general unit work and that Becky doesn't recognize or appreciate this because you don't attract attention to yourself.

Pat: Yes!

You: Becky, what would you like for Pat to do differently? Asking her to resign is not an option. Please be specific about how you would like her to change.

Pat, I ask you to think of how you would like Becky to change, understanding that asking her to leave is not an option. Please be specific.

Becky: I want Pat to let me know when she's answered lights or helped doctors find charts so I'll know that I don't have to worry about those patients or doctors. I mean, she could say something like, 'I've taken Mrs. Page to the bathroom so she should be OK for the next couple of hours. And, Drs. Stevens and Cartwright have been by and completed their charts.'

You: In other words, you want specific communication about happenings on the unit that also involve you?

Becky: Yes.

You: Pat, can you do that?

Pat: Yes.

You: Pat, how, specifically, would you like Becky to change?

Pat: I want her to stop telling me to do those things that I'm already doing without being told.

You: Can you be more specific?

Pat: I want her to stop telling me to answer lights, to get ready for doctors, and to help keep the nurses' station clean.

You: Becky, can you do that?

Becky: Yes.

You: Becky, if these changes take place, will you accept that the unit tasks *are* being done, and that you don't have to tell Pat what to do, and still feel that you're doing a good job?

Becky: Yes. It's important that people know.

You: Pat, can you increase your communications with Becky, as she has asked, and still feel that you are

Commentator: You maintained a sensitive but authoritative approach, ensured that options were acceptable and specific, and that each person got something out of it (win-win). And, you planned on follow-up to be sure the current plan would work.

doing your job competently and without direct supervision?

Pat: Yes. In fact, it should be better.

You: Thank you for your honesty, and your willingness to resolve this problem. I'd like for us to meet back here in two weeks to discuss progress on improving your relationship with each other.

And they all lived happily ever after.

THE END

Here are some suggestions for further use of *Pat and Becky*. First, copy the play for use by staff. Then, ask staff members to volunteer for each one of the four roles. Upon completion of the play, process the action. One way of doing this is to say, "Even though the parts are written for us, we're inclined to let a little bit of ourselves leak out into playing that role. I'd like to tap into that part of you that leaked out.

"Becky, did she hear you? Was she fair to you? Did you get something out of this? What did you get? Can you live with the solution? Are you and Pat going to be best friends?" (Probably not. Remember that the goal is to resolve the conflict—not to establish a friendship.) Does this take care of all your problems with Becky? NO! She has no business barking orders to *anyone*. This is not the place to address that problem.

Ask the same questions of Pat.

Ask the manager, "Were you in control? Who solved the conflict? You? Or Pat and Becky? What did you control?"

Ask the Commentator, "What were your observations, other than the words written for you?

Have fun with the play—and believe that you can do this. You really *can* do this now; you have the skills. I have seen conflicts resolved in no more time than this. It is a matter of controlling and directing the process. Write the six steps in the process on a four-by-six-inch card and keep it on the desk in front of you.

We've come to the end. Let's wrap it up.

Epilogue

Or, What Now?

We started, you and me, a long time ago with a prologue that said: This is where we're going and this is how we're going to get there.

We did it!

We established a conceptual framework, self-care, within which we honor and value the right of the other person to make decisions in her own behalf, given that she has the knowledge, ability, skills, and motivation. It is my major task as a manager and leader to provide the knowledge, ability, skills, and motivation.

We identified eight principles that would guide us as we attempt to put into practice this belief in empowering others, and we referred back to them many times, to be sure that we were being true to ourselves, to our values, to our beliefs. Our first principle provided the tone for the rest: **Principle 1: Most people want to live up to our expectations.**

Hersey and Blanchard were wise enough to develop a model of management and leadership that serves as a road map to independent, or interdependent decision making. We used their map, and internalized the belief that before I can become a supportive manager, I must first provide direction. Throughout the book we have been true to all our principles, the second of which is no less important than the first: **Principle 2: Interaction with others is more effective when we meet them where they are rather than where we want them to be.**

We added depth to what we already knew about motivation, and then integrated that learning into our examination of how to modify another person's behavior. We applied our third and fourth principles: **Principle 3: Given the knowledge, ability, skills, and motivation, people can make their own decisions in matters pertaining to their work,** and **Principle 4: We can't change anyone's behavior but our own.**

The situational, or developmental, model of management and leadership is all about change. Behavior modification is about change. We then took an intense look at just plain old change, from a personal as well as an organizational perspective. We looked at successful change, and unsuccessful change, and examined the "Why?" of each one. And, we applied our fifth principle. **Principle 5: Any effort to implement change will be met by a degree of resistance proportional to the meaning of the change to the person.**

The most important task we have as leaders is communication. We acknowledged the communication circle, then promptly put it aside and added considerable depth to our concept of effective communication. This addition ranged from an examination of the effectiveness of the parent-adult-child model of communication, to active listening, to upward communication. And, we added another principle: **Principle 6: Communication is most effective when the speaker and the audience speak the same language.**

The remainder of our time together was devoted to those persons who, for their own reasons, make our lives miserable—the difficult people. And, we really saw the practical application of **Principle 7: Most people who are difficult to deal with are responding to their own anger or fear.**

And, we brought it all together: motivation, behavior modification, communications, and difficult people, in learning about conflicts, and how to resolve conflicts between two persons who are at war with each other. We applied our final **Principle 8: When an irresistible force meets an immovable object in a clash of two** personalities, the most effective resolution is when both parties get something out of it.

Our acknowledged leaders in nursing graced us with their insights and agreed to mentor us through their words of wisdom. We are grateful for that.

Where Do I Go from Here?

This is often the question. My sincere suggestion is to do what we have done throughout our journey together—take a look at yourself. Take a couple of weeks and think about who you are; what you are doing and why that makes a difference; what your staff can expect of you; and what you expect of them. Write it down. Things look different on paper. When you are content that you have identified your core beliefs, have a discussion with your administrator to outline your goals and objectives and how you intend to get there. Then, take a deep breath and have a staff meeting: "Beginning today . . ."

Prepare for a little (a lot of?) resistance—after all, this is new behavior on your part and they have to learn to trust that you mean what you say. Then stand back! To watch your staff develop and to know that you knew they could do it; that you taught them how; that you ". . . let them sink, but never drown" (*June Bowman); that you had a hand in their growth is going to give you the same lump in your throat that I got writing this epilogue.

Thanks for spending time with me.

Bibliography

Alberti, R. E., and Emmons, M. L. *A Guide to Assertive Living: Your Perfect Right*, 4th ed. San Luis Obispo, CA: Impact Publishers, 1982.

Allison, M. A., and Allison, E. *Managing Up, Managing Down*. New York: Simon and Schuster, 1994.

Beck, C. K., et al, eds. *Mental Health-Psychiatric Nursing*, 2d ed. St. Louis: C. V. Mosby, 1988.

Benefield, L. E. "Motivating Professional Staff." *Nursing Administration Quarterly* 12, no. 4 (1988): 57–62.

Bennis, Warren G. *On Becoming a Leader*. Menlo Park: Addison-Wesley, 1990.

Bennis, Warren G. et al. *The Planning of Change*, 4th ed. New York: Holt, Rinehart and Winston, 1985.

Blanchard, Ken. *Managing the Journey: Understanding and Implementing Change*. Escondido, CA: Blanchard Training and Development, 1993.

Bower, S. A. and Bower, G. H. *Asserting Yourself*, 2d ed. Reading, MA: Addison-Wesley, 1991.

Burley-Allen, Madelyn. *Managing Assertively: How to Improve Your People Skills*. New York: John Wiley and Sons, 1983.

Chase, J. "Nurse Manager Competencies." *Journal of Nursing Administration* 24, no. 4S (1994): 56–64.

Covey, Stephen R. *The 7 Habits of Highly Effective People*. New York: Simon and Schuster, 1993.

Crawley, J. *Constructive Conflict Management*. San Diego: Pfeiffer and Company, 1992.

Dolan, T. C. "Perspectives: Sharpening Your Interpersonal Skills." *Healthcare Executive*, July/August, 1993.

Gordon, Thomas. *Leader Effectiveness Training*. Columbus, OH: Charles E. Merrill, 1984.

Grohar-Murray, M. E. and DiCroce, H. R. *Leadership and Management in Nursing*. Norwalk: Appleton & Lange, 1992.

Hammer, M. and Champy, J. *Reengineering the Corporation: A Manifesto for Business Revolution*. New York: HarperCollins Publishers, 1993.

Hersey, Paul and Blanchard, Ken. *Management of Organizational Behavior: Utilizing Human Resources*, 6th ed. Englewood Cliffs: Prentice-Hall, 1992.

Heifetz, M. L. *Leading Change, Overcoming Chaos*. Berkeley, CA: Ten Speed Press, 1993.

Hodgetts, Richard M. *Management of Organizational Behavior: Theory, Process and Practice*, 5th ed. Philadelphia: W. B. Saunders, 1989.

Huppe, Frank F. *Successful Delegation*. Hawthorne, NJ: Career Press, 1994.

Kawamota, K. "Nursing Leadership: To Thrive in a World of Change." *Nursing Administration Quarterly* 18, no. 3 (1994):1–6.

Kerrigan, K. "Decision Making in Today's Complex Environment." *Nursing Administration Quarterly* 15, no. 4 (1991):1–5.

Manion, J. "Understanding the Seven Stages of Change." *American Journal of Nursing* 95, no. 4 (1995): 41–43.

Marano, H. E. "Big, Bad Bully." *Psychology Today* 28, no. 5 (1995): 50–56, 62–63.

Marano, H. E. "When the Boss Is a Bully." *Psychology Today* 28, no. 5 (1995): 58–61.

McKibbin, S. "The Paradox of Change." *Hospitals and Health Networks*, January 20, 1995, 40–42.

Meighan, M. M. "The Most Important Characteristics of Nursing Leaders as Identified by Staff Nurses." *Nursing Administration Quarterly* 15, no. 1 (1990): 63–69.

Morin, W. J *Silent Sabotage*. New York: American Management Association, 1995.

Nakata, J. A. and Saylor, C. "Management Style and Staff Nurse Satisfaction in a Changing Environment." *Nursing Administration Quarterly* 18, no. 3 (1994): 51–57.

Neubauer, J. "The Learning Network: Leadership Development for the Next Millennium." *Journal of Nursing Administration* 25, no. 2 (1995): 23–32.

Newstrom, John W. and Davis, Keith. *Organizational Behavior: Human Behavior at Work*, 9th ed. New York: McGraw-Hill, 1993.

Perley, M. J. and Raab, A. "Beyond Shared Governance: Restructuring Care Delivery for Self-Managing Work Teams." *Nursing Administration Quarterly* 19, no. 1 (1994):12–20.

Peters, T. *Thriving on Chaos*. New York: HarperCollins Publishers, 1987.

Peters, T. *The Tom Peters Seminar: Crazy Times Call for Crazy Organizations*. New York: Vintage Books, 1994.

Rees, Fran. *How to Lead Work Teams: Facilitation Skills*. San Diego: Pfeiffer and Company, 1991.

Rogers, Carl R. and Freiberg, H. Jerome. *Freedom to Learn*, 3d ed., Columbus, OH: Charles E. Merrill, 1994.

Scott, J. S. and Rantz, M. "Change Champions at the Grassroots Level : Practice Innovation Using Team Process." *Nursing Administration Quarterly* 18, no. 3 (1994): 7–17.

Senge, P. M. *The Fifth Discipline: the Art and Practice of the Learning Organization.* New York: Currency Doubleday, 1990.

Senge, P. M., et al. *The Fifth Discipline Fieldbook.* New York: Currency Doubleday, 1994.

Senteny. W. K. *Basic Supervision.* Trafalgar, IN: Independent Management, Inc., 1992.

Skinner, B. F. Beyond Freedom and Dignity. New York: Alfred A. Knopf, 1971.

Skinner, M. D. "Getting to X." *Nursing Administration Quarterly* 18, no. 3 (1994): 58–63.

Spiker, B. K., et al. "Managing Change in the Health Care Industry." *Viewpoint* 23, no 4 (fall, 1994).

Strasen, L. "Reengineering Hospitals Using the 'Function Follows Form' Model." *Journal of Nursing Administration* 24, no. 12 (1994): 59–63.

Stuart, Gail W. and Sundeen, Sandra J. *Principles and Practice of Psychiatric Nursing* 4th ed. St. Louis: C. V. Mosby, 1990.

Tappen, R. M. *Nursing Leadership and Management: Concepts and Practice,* 3d ed. Philadelphia: F. A. Davis, 1994.

Tracy, D. *10 Steps to Empowerment.* New York: William Morrow, 1990.

Triolo, P. K., et al. "Layoff Survivor Sickness: Minimizing the Sequelae of Organizational Transformation." *Journal of Nursing Administration,* 25, no. 3 (1995): 56–63.

Wilson, Holly S. *Psychiatric Nursing,* 4th ed. Menlo Park: Addison-Wesley, 1992.

Young, S. W., et al. "Excellence in Leadership through Organizational Development." *Nursing Administration Quarterly* 12, no. 4 (1988): 69–77.

INDEX

Accommodation, 178
Accountability, 20
Achievement
　delegation and, 30
　human motivational needs and, 141
Acknowledging the child, 126
Active listening; *see* Listening
Administrators
　communications with, 130–131, 135–137
　talking their language, 131–133
Adult model
　adult ego state, 115–116
　Karpman triangle and, 171–172
　responding to aggressive attacks from,
　　154–159
　of transactional analysis, 109–110
Age, listening and, 121
Aggression
　anger and, 139–140, 147
　case studies of, 152–154
　characteristics of, 144, 146–147
　confronting, 154–159
　dealing with, 147
　parent-adult-child model and, 153–159
　targeting others and, 151–152, 154
Alberti, Robert E., 153
Alessandra, T., 119
Allison, E., 134
Allison, M. A., 134
Anger
　aggression and, 139–140, 147
　assertiveness and, 141, 172
　characteristics of, 140–142
　difficult people and, 139–140, 192
　frustration and, 142–143
　passive-aggressive, 144–147, 173
　physiological effect of, 140–141
　psychological response to, 141
　rage, 148–149
　resentment and, 140, 173
　responses to, 173
　as search, 142
　understanding, 139–140
Anxiety, created by changes, 88–89

Approach-approach conflict, 176
Assertiveness
　aggressive attacks and, 154–159
　anger and, 142, 173
　avoiding "you" in conversations, 159
　in communications, 155–161, 173
　intimidation and, 161–162
　learning, 160–161
　premises of, 155
Attention, and selective listening, 123
Authoritarian/directive role, leadership
　and, 3–9
Avoidance, conflict and resolution,
　176–178, 180

Bass, Thelma A., 121
Behavior modification, 57–74
　assertive interactions and, 158, 160
　consistency and, 29, 70
　principles applied to, 73
　problem resolution and, 69–70
　reinforcement and, 58–62, 63–64
　worksheet for, 74
Behaviors
　changing, 64–69, 158, 160, 192
　controlling vs. extinguishing, 61–62
　identifying negative, 64–65, 71, 72
　motivation and, 49, 58–61
Bell curve, staff capabilities charted as,
　26–27
Belonging, 141
Berne, Eric, 108–110
Beyond Freedom and Dignity, 57–58
Bibliography, 195–197
Blanchard, Ken, 2, 30
Boundaries, 7, 11–12, 15–17, 24
Bowman, June C., xi, 17, 124, 175, 193

Caring, 29
Case studies
　of aggressive attacks, 152–154
　of organizational change, 101–103

Case studies—(*Cont.*)
  in passivity, 144–146
  redirecting staff members, 31–40, 64–73
Champy, J., 14
Chance, expectancy theory and, 49–50
Change, 75–105
  anxiety about, 88–89
  case study of disastrous, 103–104
  components of, 78
  coping and, 89–92
  costs as source of potential, 81–83
  evaluating options for, 83–84
  implementing, 86–87, 97–98
  as loss, 77, 96
  organizational, 96–99
  personal and organizational models of,
    99–101
  personal process of, 76–96
  PERT charts, 84–85
  recovery from, 89
  regression and, 95
  resistance to, 77, 78, 96, 103, 192
  Rogers' principles of learning and, 94
  stress and, 91–92
  structuring with information, 79–85
Changing behaviors, 64–65, 158, 160
Child
  acknowledging emotions, 127
  aggressive behavior and, 153–159
  transactional analysis and, 109–110
Circle of self, 66, 77
Cognitive dissonance, 154
Collaboration, as conflict resolution, 179,
  180
Communicating at Work, 119
Communication for Health Professionals, 121
Communications, 107–137; *see also*
  Listening
  active listening, 124–128
  with administrators, 133–137
  assertiveness and, 155–161, 173
  avoiding "you" in conversations, 159
  with difficult people, 173–174
  effective, 96, 103, 104–105, 135, 192
  about feelings, 156–158
  goals for, 107–108
  leadership and, 2
  shock effect and, 159–160
  speaking the same language, 130–131,
    135, 192

Communication wheel, 107–108
Competition, as conflict resolution,
  179–180
Complementary transactions, 113
Compromise, 179
Conceptual framework; *see* Principles
Conflict, types of, 175–178
Conflict resolution, 175–189
  effective, 192
  identifying differences in, 182
  role playing and, 183–189
  structure and process of, 181–183
  types of, 176–180
Consistency, 29, 70
  manipulators and, 164, 172–173
Contingency plans, for out-of-control
  people, 148–149
Control
  behaviors to gain, 58–59
  manipulators and, 165–167, 172–173
  as a motivating factor, 73
Cost-effectiveness, as source of change,
  81–83
Covey, Stephen, 120
Crisis theory, 89
Critical parent, of transactional analysis,
  109–110
Crossed transactions, 114

Decision making
  coaching and, 12–13
  dumb decisions and, 14–15
  principles applied to, 27, 35, 55, 191
  process of, 131–133
  staff as decision makers, 8–9, 12–13,
    15–17, 24–25, 192
Delegate level
  personal power and, 112
  situational leadership models and,
    18–25, 30, 46
  transactional analysis and, 111–112
Delegating responsibilities, 18–25
Denial, change and, 77
Destructive child, 110
Deviled eggs, recipe for, 56
Differences, conflictual, 182
Difficult people, 139–174
  anger, 139–140
  communications with, 173–174

Difficult people—(*Cont.*)
  dealing with, 173–174
  manipulators as, 140, 162–173
  responding to own anger and fear, 192
Dissatisfiers, motivation and, 43–44

Education, listening and, 121
Edwards, Frances M., xi, 4
Effective communications, 96, 103,
  104–105, 133–137, 192
Effective listening; *see* Listening
Effort, expectancy theory and, 49–50, 66–67
Emmons, Michael L., 155
Employees, managing, 8–9
Expectancy theory, 49–56
  chance and, 49–50
  effort and, 49–50, 66–67
  high and low achievers, 54–55
  rewards, 50, 64–70, 71–72
Expectations
  achieving, 3, 191
  knowledge, ability, and skills and,
    10–11
  and motivation, 44–46
Exposure, selective listening and, 122–123

Failure, advantages of, 14–15
Fairness, 29
Feelings, communicating, 156–158
Fight-or-flight response, anger and, 140,
  173
Firing employees, during probationary
  period, 9
Firmness, 29
Fixed rate of reinforcement, 58–59, 61
Fixed ratio of reinforcement, 59–60
Focus, maintaining, 167–168
Form, function and, 99
Frankl, Viktor, 41
Frustration, anger and, 142–143
Function, and form, 99

Games, for manipulators, 168–169
Games People Play, 108–110
Goals
  blocked, 142
  implementing, 97–98
  organizational change and, 97

Guide to Assertive Living, A, 155
Gunnysacking, 144–146

Half-way parties, 95
Hammer, M., 14
Happy child, of transactional analysis, 110
Hersey, Paul, 2, 30
Herzberg, Frederick, 43
High achievers, 54–55
Human motivational needs, 41–43, 141–142
Hunsaker, P., 119
Huppe, Dr. Frank F., 19–20

Impartiality, in conflict resolution, 181
Implementing change, 86–87, 97–98
Implementing mission statements, 6–7
Information
  gathering about conflicts, 182
  structuring change with, 79–85
Initiators, manipulation and, 167
Interactions
  delegating, 18–25, 30, 46
  effective, 3, 33, 73, 103, 133–137, 192
  participating, 13–18, 30, 46
  selling, 10–13, 30, 46, 70
  telling, 2–9, 30, 46
  transactional analysis of, 110–112
Intimidation, assertiveness and, 161–162

Jenkins, Judith M., xi, 101–102
Job descriptions, 3–5
Johnson, Jean T., xi, 63–64
Jones, Mary Lou, xi, 27–28, 90–91, 174

Karpman triangle, 170–172
Kerrigan, K., 12–13
Knowledge, change and, 91–92

Language
  business, 131–133
  using shared, 130–131
Leadership; *see also* Situational leadership
  model
  authoritarian/directive role, 3–9
  delegating responsibilities, 18–25

Leadership—(*Cont.*)
foundations for, 2, 3–6
for managers, 3–28
model for, 1–28
skills, 4–5
staff participation, 13–18
supporting change and, 83–84
teach/coach role, 10–13
Learning
assertiveness, 160–161
facilitating, 92, 94–95
gap in knowledge and, 91–92
Rogers' principles of, 94
under stress, 92–96
Limits, setting, 167–168
Listening, 119–130; *see also*
Communications
acknowledging the child, 127
adult communications with, 126
factors affecting, 121–122
goals for, 121
need for, 120–121
practice sessions for, 129–130
selective, 122–124
skills for active, 124–130
Loss, recognizing change as, 77, 96
Low achievers, 54–55

Managers
change and, 78, 83–84, 89–91
delegating, 18–26
effective communications, 87, 130–137
firing employees, 9
leadership model for, 3–28
learning the administrator's priorities, 134
listening and, 120–121
positive reinforcement techniques, 63–64
staff's expectations of, 29
tips for, 95
trusting, 14–15
Managing Up, Managing Down, 135
Manipulation, 162–173
characteristics of, 162–163
dealing with, 168–169
games and, 168–169
initiators and responders, 167
problems with, 128

Manipulation—(*Cont.*)
setting and testing limits, 167–168
understanding, 140
Maslow, Abraham, 30
human motivational needs, 41–43, 141–142
McDonald, John C., xi, 130–131
Mission statements, 3–5
implementing, 6–7
organizational change and, 79–80, 97
sample, 5–6
supporting, 10
Money
as motivator, 44, 51–52
as a satisfier, 52–54
Monkey on the Back game, 168–169
Morale, reporting "V" and, 134–135
Morin, William J., 14–15, 80
Motivation, 41–56, 57–73; *see also*
Reinforcement
behavior and, 49, 58–61
control as, 73
correcting negative, 63–64
expectancy theory and, 49–56
expectations and, 44–46
human needs and, 41–43, 141–142
money as, 44, 51–54
satisfiers and dissatisfiers, 43–44
shaping behavior with, 58–61
Theory X, 41
Theory Y, 41–43
Motivators
praising, 44–46
working for, 54–55

Nurses, implementing mission statements, 6–7
Nursing, self-care concept of, ix–x, 1–2, 192
Nurturing parent, of transactional analysis, 109–110

Objectives; *see* Goals
Orem, Dorothea, ix–x, 1
Organizational change, 96–99
components of, 96–97
effective, 101–103
organizational charts, 98
and personal change, 99–101
planning for, 100–101

Organizational charts, 98
Outcomes, as element of cost-effectiveness, 81–83
Out-of-control people, rage and, 148

Paper airplane making, learning under stress and, 92–96
Parent-adult-child model
    aggressive behavior and, 153–159
    of transactional analysis, 109–110
Participate level
    personal power and, 112
    situational leadership models and, 13–18, 30, 46
    transactional analysis and, 111
Passive-aggressive people, 144, 146–147
Passivity
    anger and, 144, 173
    case studies in, 144–146
    gunnysacking and, 145–146
Peak experiences, 48
Perception, selective listening and, 123
Persecutors, victims and, 170–172
Persistence, managers and, 95
Personal change, 76–96
    and organizational change, 99–101
Personal characteristics, evaluating, 149–152
Personality clashes, 178
Personal power, 154, 158
PERT charts, 84–85
Peters, Tom, 14
Physiological conditions
    effect of anger on, 140–141
    human motivation and, 30, 141–142
    listening and, 122
Pigeons, Skinner's experiments with, 58–61
Planning
    delegating and, 21
    for effective change, 100–101
Policies and procedures, 4
Positional power, tell and sell levels and, 112
Positive reinforcement; see Reinforcement
Practice sessions, for active listening, 129–130
Praising
    as motivator, 44–46
    specific, 32–33

Prater, Judith B., xi, 45–46, 63
Principles; see also Situational leadership model
    applying, 27
    behavior modification and, 73
    for dealing with difficult people, 173–174
    for decision making, 27, 35, 55, 191
    effective conflict resolution, 192
    effective interactions, 3, 33, 73, 103, 133–137, 192
    for empowering others, ix–xi, 191–193
    expectations as, 3, 44–46, 191
    resistance to change, 96, 104
    respecting other's views as, 96, 130–131, 135, 192
    of self-care nursing, ix–x, 1–2, 192
    situational leadership model, 1–28
Probationary period, firing employees during, 9
Problem resolution, behavior modification and, 69–70
Process
    for conflict resolution, 181–183
    for decision making, 131–133
Psychological response, to anger, 140
Punishment, 60–62

Quality, cost-effectiveness and, 81–83

Rage, 146–147
Recognition, 30, 31–32
Recovery, from change, 89
Redirecting staff members, 29
    behavior modification and, 70
    case studies of, 31–40, 64–73
    conflict resolution and, 181–183
    effective interactions, 3, 33, 73, 103, 133–137, 192
Regression, at the halfway point, 95
Reinforcement
    behavior modification and, 58–62, 63–69
    changing behavior with, 64–69, 72
    fixed rate of, 58–59, 61
    fixed ratio of, 59–60
    rewards as, 64–69, 72
    schedules for modifying behavior, 61–63

Reinforcement—(*Cont.*)
    used by managers, 63–64
    variable ratios of, 60–62
Relationships, assertive communications
    and, 156
Rescuers, 169–172
Resentment, anger and, 140, 173
Resistance, to change, 77, 78, 96, 103, 104,
    192
Responders, manipulation and, 167
Retention, selective, 123
Rewards
    expectancy theory and, 50, 64–70,
    71–72
    reinforcement and, 64–69, 72
    withdrawing, 61–61
Rogers, Carl, 41, 92, 94–95
Role playing, 183–189

Safety and security, 30, 140
Satisfiers, 43–44, 53–55
Selective listening, 122–124
Self-actualization, 46–47
Self-care nursing, ix–x, 1–2, 192
Self-esteem, 30, 141
Self-evaluation, 147–152
Sell level
    behavioral changes and, 70
    positional power and, 112
    principles of self-care nursing and, 10
    selling ideas to staff, 10–11
    situational leadership models and,
        10–13, 30, 46
    transactional analysis and, 111
Sensitivity, in conflict resolution, 181
7 Habits of Highly Effective People, The, 120
Sex, listening and, 121
Shock effect, 159–160
Silent Sabotage (Morin), 14–15
Situational leadership model
    assertive communications and, 156
    delegate level, 18–25, 30, 46
    effective interactions and, 3, 33, 73, 103,
        136–137, 192
    participate level, 13–18, 30, 46
    sell level, 10–13, 30, 46
    tell level, 2–9, 30, 46
    transactional analysis and, 110–112
Skinner, B. F., 57–62

Smith, Voncile M., 121
Social acceptance, sell level and, 30
Social and economic background, listening
    and, 122
Speaking the same language, principle of,
    96, 130–131, 135, 192
Staffing, goals and objectives for, 98
Staff members
    capabilities of, 26–28
    communications with managers,
        130–131
    as decision makers, 12–13, 15–17, 24–25,
        192
    delegating to, 18–21
    need for recognition, 31–32
    questions about change, 87
    redirecting and reprimanding, 29
    selling ideas to, 10–13
    setting boundaries for, 8–9
    supporting, 13–18, 22–24
    values for managers, 29
Status, listening and, 122
Strategic plans, 97
Strategies, for manipulators, 168–169
Strengths, 149–152
Stress, 91–96
Structure
    and change, 89–92
    conflict resolution and, 181–183
    providing during change, 79–85
Substituting behaviors, 67–68
Support
    for staff members, 13–18, 22–24
    transactional analysis and, 112
Surgeons, 149

Targeting others, 151–152, 154
Teach/coach role, 10–13
Team effort, organizational change and,
    101–103
Tell level
    positional power and, 112
    principles of self-care nursing and, 3
    situational leadership models and, 2–9,
        30, 46
    transactional analysis and, 110–111
Testing limits, manipulators and, 167–168
Theory X, motivation and, 41
Theory Y, motivation and, 41–43

Transactional analysis, 108–118
   kinds of transactions, 113–116
   parent-adult-child model, 109–110
   sample communications for, 116–118
Trust, 14–15, 80

Ulterior transactions, 114–115

Values, 3–5
Variable ratios of reinforcement, 60–62
Victims, 169–172
Vroom, V. H., 49–50

Weaknesses, 149–152
Who Owns the Problem game, 168–169

ABOUT THE AUTHOR

Kathleen (Katie) O'Sullivan Mott, M.S., R.N., is founder and principal of O'Sullivan Communications, a consulting firm that specializes in leadership, communications, and managing change.

Katie returned to school when her youngest son was 12 years old, and refers to herself as a "middle-age retread." She has had experience as a staff nurse, charge nurse, department head, program planner, nurse researcher, clinical specialist, consultant, instructor, and in community development and grant writing. She is the recipient of numerous awards and honors, is a member of Tennessee Nurses Association, Sigma Theta Tau, and is listed in *Who's Who in American Nursing* and *2,000 Notable America Women*.

She currently lives in Nashville, Tennessee, with her trophy husband of many years, and considers herself fortunate that most of her family lives nearby. When she isn't conducting seminars, writing, or consulting, Katie can be found in the kitchen. She also loves to cook.